A PALPABLE GOD

REYNOLDS PRICE

A PALPABLE
GOD

THIRTY STORIES TRANSLATED FROM THE BIBLE
WITH AN ESSAY ON THE ORIGINS
AND LIFE OF NARRATIVE

THE AKADINE PRESS

1997

A Palpable God

A COMMON READER EDITION published 1997 by The Akadine Press, Inc., by arrangement with Scribner, an imprint of Simon & Schuster, Inc.

A COMMON READER EDITION and fountain colophon are trademarks of The Akadine Press, Inc.

ISBN 1-888173-07-6

FOR

KATHERINE LAIRD ELLIS
NICHOLAS MICHAEL JORDAN
KATHERINE REYNOLDS PRICE
AND
MARIE ELIZABETH PRICE

CONTENTS

Remember the advise of *Nazianzene. It is a grievous thing* (or dangerous) *to neglect a great faire, and to seeke to make markets afterwards.* . . .

> "The Translators to the Reader,"
> King James Version

A PALPABLE GOD

A SINGLE MEANING

NOTES ON
THE ORIGINS
AND LIFE
OF NARRATIVE

A NEED to tell and hear stories is essential to the species *Homo sapiens*—second in necessity apparently after nourishment and before love and shelter. Millions survive without love or home, almost none in silence; the opposite of silence leads quickly to narrative, and the sound of story is the dominant sound of our lives, from the small accounts of our days' events to the vast incommunicable constructs of psychopaths.

It is odd then that nothing is known of the origins of narrative and that few serious attempts have been made to speculate on those origins—the conditions (supernatural, psychic, physiological, or social) which resulted in the development in man of a story-telling response to inner and outer events.

Of course, if we assume that narrative is specifically a human function, then we confess that nothing firm is known of the origin of the species itself. But the assumption that narrative is purely human is decidedly shaky—there is increasing evidence that apes, whales, and porpoises have elaborate narrative needs and powers and that almost all animals possess systems of communication, means for the transfer of information at least if not narrative—ants, bees, birds, snails? bacteria? That is a later question however—of the difference between narrative and information.

It is not immediately clear what questions should come first in any inquiry into sources, possible causes, of a need so universal and so ruthlessly pursued by seductive geniuses, paralyzing bores, deaf-mutes, madmen—almost all human creatures—but a question very near the beginning would be *When did man develop language?*

There is no answer yet. Paleoanthropologists change their minds annually after digesting each summer's African digs, but recent information available to laymen suggests that manlike creatures (*Homo erectus*) existed as early as three and three-quarter million years ago.[1] And some recent disputed evidence would push linguistic ability in man, or at least the presence on the brain of the speech-essential Broca's area, back to between two and three million years ago.[2] Yet our oldest known samples of linguistic writing are only some five thousand-five hundred years old—considerable room for guessing. Linguists have obliged with centuries of speculation on the origin of language— divine gift (the theory of most ancient peoples and a few modern students), imitation of nonhuman sound (what Max Müller called the Bow-wow theory), response to pain or intense feeling (the Pooh-pooh theory), natural accompaniment to common acts of labor (the Yo-he-ho theory), mystic correspondence be-

1. *New York Times*, April 12, 1975, p. 29; March 9, 1976, p. 14.
2. *New York Times*, April 21, 1976, p. 33.

tween sound and sense (the Ding-dong theory), inevitable result of brain structure, and on and on: the literature is immense. In the light of what follows, one guess deserves notice—Otto Jespersen's suggestion that

> the genesis of language is not to be sought in the prosaic, but in the poetic side of life; the source of speech is not gloomy seriousness, but merry play and youthful hilarity. And among the emotions which were most powerful in eliciting outbursts of music and of song, love must be placed in the front rank.[1]

A student of narrative who enters linguistic speculation is likely to feel soon, however, that while story and language are now solidly bound, they may not have been so for long on the scale of human time. He may even begin to wonder if the need to narrate was not in itself crucial to the origin of language—*to narrate* as distinct from *to inform*.

The informative and protective advantages of an ability for verbal narration are obvious, and it does not require the anecdotal etiology of "A Dissertation upon Roast Pig" to imagine other pressures to narrate upon mute creatures. Modern human beings tell themselves stories well before they possess speech or substantial experience of the world—all healthy babies dream. Given the proclivity of adults in most societies to value and fear and share their dreams, that pressure alone may have been powerful in the drive for speech, as it still seems to be. (Dogs dream but have not yet spoken in sizable numbers, though the fact that they are such

1. Otto Jespersen, *Language: Its Nature, Development, and Origin* (London, 1928) p. 433.

new artifacts of man's genetic mischief absolves them of laziness—if not of the conscious frustration which dog-lovers suspect their pets to experience at the inability.) Few babies however can have launched their maiden speeches with "Falling!" or "Starving!" or "Dark!"—perhaps the common subjects of their dreams. To be sure, parents seldom prompt with such words; yet babies hear adults use and reuse thousands of words from large vocabularies. Why do they generally choose to begin with a family name?—Ma-ma, Pa-pa.

—Because there are needs which result in speech but are not needs *for* speech. Language is vehicle, almost never destination. So the first question in a search for the roots of story would not be *When did man speak?*, but it might be *Why?* The second would then be *What did he say?*

We have scant evidence, from any known cultures, to answer either. Oddly, few mythologies offer elaborate explanations of the origins and early nature of speech. The Egyptian god Thoth spoke the words which created the world; the Hindu goddess Vak created the world by saying "Bhu"; in Plato's *Cratylus* Socrates affirms that the gods gave all things their proper names and that Hermes conveyed those names to men; numerous peoples preserve explanations of the diversity of languages similar to the story of the Tower of Babel. But the fullest and most thoughtful account is that which begins the Hebrew Bible—Genesis 2, the story of the start of what is now western civilization.

Adam breaks silence first, like most children, to name his companions—

> *God Yahweh molded from the ground each*
> *beast of the field and each bird of the skies*
> *and brought them to the man to see what he*
> *might call it and whatever the man called*
> *each living soul was its name. So the man*
> *gave names to all cattle, birds of the skies,*
> *and each beast of the field.*

That initial speech fails. We are told at once "But for man he did not find a helper as his mate," and the creation of woman follows to remedy the lack. In Book VIII of *Paradise Lost*, Milton's Adam expands convincingly upon the lightly sketched but richly implicit dilemma of Genesis—

> *Thou [God] hast provided all things: but with*
>   *mee*
> *I see not who partakes. In solitude*
> *What happiness, who can enjoy alone,*
> *Or all enjoying, what contentment find?*

And to God's subsequent argument that He is single also, Adam replies keenly,

> *But Man by number is to manifest*
> *His single imperfection, and beget*
> *Like of his like, his Image multipli'd,*
> *In unity defective. . . .*
>
> > (VIII, 363–366, 422–425)

Adam spoke, in Genesis and *Paradise Lost*, not to assert ability or dominion but to search for "a helper as his mate." Our central myth of the origin of language says that man invented speech to define his solitude, to confess his tragic incompleteness. (From Genesis we gather that Adam also invented narrative; when God hunts out the human pair after their fall, Adam says, "I heard Your voice in the garden and feared, since I'm naked, and hid myself"—a chronologically consecutive account of more than one past event, with attention to cause and self-defense: thus a narrative.)

So while myths of the origin of speech are provocative, they will not bear the weight of a search for bedrock. What is needed is a record of early human speech; obviously there is none, though there are intriguing modern fragments which look like survivors but promise more than they tell—incantations in what appear to be, but almost certainly are not, abstract sounds:

> *Da a da da*
> *Da a da da*
> *Da a da da*
> *Da kata kai.*

> *Ded o ded o*
> *Ded o ded o*
> *Ded o ded o*
> *Da kata kai.*[1]

Recent studies of primate communication also offer numerous openings for luxuriant analogy; continuing investigation of the physiology of brain and mind (and such humbler matters as the evolution of teeth, tongue, and jaw) may yield leads; so may further studies of primitive languages, further archeological and evolu-

1. Aboriginal rain song, Australia. Caillois and Lambert, *Trésor de la Poésie Universelle* (Paris, 1958) p. 25.

tionary findings. But anything resembling an answer evades us and may always do so.

Whenever man first spoke, whatever he said, he seems to have waited millions of years to make records. The earliest known "written" records seem to be the engraved bones and stones which Alexander Marshack has studied so freshly and convincingly—upper paleolithic remains from Africa and Europe, some perhaps thirty-five thousand years old.[1] Marshack believes and argues strongly that they demonstrate sophisticated and partially decipherable methods for calculating and recording lunar phases and perhaps menstrual and pregnancy cycles and for symbolizing the elements of hunt and vegetation stories and rites. Hundreds of such examples are already known, and they push the history of both writing and narrative back ten thousand years beyond the famous cave paintings of France and Spain (the nature of whose narrative content, if any, is hotly debated).

Yet, to repeat, man as a recognizably distinct animal is perhaps four million years old. His use of a fairly complex range of tools is nearly as old; his control and use of fire is perhaps eight hundred thousand years old—and each of these skills tempts us to infer some form of oral communication, if only for the teaching of skills to others. Our oldest samples of writing in pictographic and alphabetical characters are only some five thousand years old; and our oldest narratives (*Gilgamesh* and a few other Near-Eastern stories) were recorded as recently as 2500 B.C., though there is reason to think they existed orally well before. Thus the

1. Alexander Marshack, *The Roots of Civilization* (New York, 1972).

known history of narrative begins roughly five-sixths of the way through what may be the *life* of narrative. The early stories which we call primitive come after millions of years of practice; they are intensely sophisticated products, though the conditions from which they proceeded may have resembled early man's so closely as to make the later stories much like his, in aim at least. Still, we know nothing of the causes and early career of a force so powerful in most daily lives. Can there be fruitful guesses? Why try?

I'll speak personally. Eight years ago I arrived, age thirty-five, at the traditional midroad of fatigue, choice, and question. The less private questions concerned my work. I'd published five books, all of them narrative; and while they'd been received with the rewarding if not smothering warmth that awaits complicated but communicative fiction in a prosperous country of two hundred-twenty million (only some few thousand of whom are committed readers of more than simple tales), I found myself questioning an impulse which had moved me since early childhood and which for almost twenty years had seemed a nearly central, surely permanent one. Could I go on for decades maybe, laboring to tell complex narratives to shrinking audiences? (the critically fashionable fiction of the late sixties was either urban-hectic or academic-experimental; it had not then become as clear as it since has to publishers, critics, or English professors that paying customers for those brands of chic would not stay amused for long). Whatever the difficulties of some of my work, I'd always felt that my own impulse—starting as it did among beloved kin who were not readers—had been toward simplicity, clarity, availability. At thirty-five I was not only doubting that such power was any longer possible to a complex narrator (as it had been to the writers on whom my adolescent ambition was formed: Dickens, Tolstoy, Twain, Hemingway)—I was also asking why I'd started at all in such an odd trade. Or landed in it; I'd started as a painter. In the midst of such questions, and while writing perhaps my least available stories, I found myself turning with increasing frequency to something new and strange—literal translations of short, almost blindingly lucid Bible stories.

They had not been the first stories I knew—both my parental families were ceaseless hives of oral narrative, and my earliest narrative memory is purely visual: my bedridden paternal grandmother slapping my own mother as she bent to kiss her—but they were the earliest I remember encountering in print. That same grandmother gave me *Wonderful Stories of the Bible* by Josephine Pollard when I was three—stories of Adam and Eve, Noah, Abraham and Isaac, Jacob and his sons, Moses, Samson, Saul, David and Jonathan, Solomon, Elijah, Daniel, and Esther. When I was four my parents, who were religious but not churchly, gave me Hurlbut's *Story of the Bible*—an essentially complete, surprisingly unlaundered version of Old and New Testaments, lavish with illustrations from nineteenth-century German art: none of your fumigated Sunday-school confections but credible ancient orientals, hairy and aromatic. Years before I could read, and I was seldom read to, I studied the pictures and built my own stories on the rapid summaries extorted from my parents. The two pictures I recall as favorites had tragic or violent implications—young Isaac bearing his own funeral pyre up a hill behind his father and young

David hacking off the vanquished giant's head. I don't recall any fascination with gentler scenes—Jesus and children, the Good Shepherd and his sheep—though I do recall numerous pensive visits to the picture of Jesus raising the dead little girl (the magnet there was not the great feat but the unvarnished news that children were serious people and could die). Once I could read, I adjusted my versions to the textual norm and turned to other stories, though the Bible stories stayed in my head; and in a pious adolescence, the stories of Jesus surfaced again as straws in the dense hormonal maelstrom. The second sizable narrative I wrote was a play about the Magi (age thirteen—the first was a play about Queen Isabella); and a freshman course in Bible was one of the lights of my undergraduate years. But aside from a permanent interest in the hidden life of Jesus, I'd made no continuing resort to the central narratives of my culture.

Here I was however at age thirty-five like a well-fed, air-conditioned anchorite, studying the actual words of the stories, struggling to haul them into true modern English—first, Abraham and Isaac; then Jacob and the angel; then the risen Jesus and the fishing disciples. I didn't know Hebrew and, at first, very little Greek but worked from literal scholarly versions toward my own bare likenesses. Why, conceivably?

First, after years of planning, I'd begun to feel ready at last to work on a long novel. At that point in the late sixties, I thought of the project as a kind of realistic allegory of my own peculiar relation to my father; and my first translation, the sacrifice of Isaac, was a conscious calisthenic for the novel. I even went further and wrote a series of meditations on the narrative implications of Rembrandt's four pictures of the scene.[1] (My father was seriously alcoholic in the six years of marriage before my birth; when both my mother and I were endangered in a difficult labor, he made a vow to quit his drinking if both of us lived; we did and he quit. I was told of the vow by the time I was five and from then on saw myself in stronger light as a pledge, a hostage with more than normal duties and perils.) So while I was still a ways from starting the novel, the early translations did whet my interest and force me to dwell on the tight range of actions and characters which has proved of any enduring interest or use to the species—family dependencies and internal revolts, tribal war against unrelated enemies, personal revenge, single combat or union with a god.

The second reason is one that doesn't discuss well. In a hard time I was turning to the inscribed bases of beliefs which had supported me and my family. The stories I was choosing were the stories I needed; and the effort to bring those inscriptions over three or four millennia, faithfully and cleanly, seemed as potent a talisman as any. As I survived the time, began to write the novel, and continued the translations, I began to see that they were not only protective but instructive. I suspected I was learning, or relearning none too soon, essential facts about my trade—facts which made the long job move more easily than any previous; facts which slowly came to seem laws, visible there near what seemed both the roots of the hunger for story and of story itself. The root of story sprang from need—need for companionship and consolation by a creature as

1. Reynolds Price, "Four Abrahams, Four Isaacs by Rembrandt" in *Things Themselves* (New York, 1972) p. 260.

vulnerable, four million years ago and now, as any protozoan in a warm brown swamp. The need is not for the total consolation of narcotic fantasy—our own will performed in airless triumph—but for credible news that our lives proceed in order toward a pattern which, if tragic here and now, is ultimately pleasing in the mind of a god who sees a totality and *at last* enacts His will. We crave nothing less than perfect story; and while we chatter or listen all our lives in a din of craving—jokes, anecdotes, novels, dreams, films, plays, songs, half the words of our days—we are satisfied only by the one short tale we feel to be true: *History is the will of a just god who knows us.*

All these motives and no doubt others remained in force for eight or nine years—still do in fact since, while a piece of that novel is finished, other pieces are in sight; life is never scarce on quandaries, and all questions continue. Meanwhile, they've produced this collection of stories—perhaps not quite the oldest surviving but the oldest which bear directly on our lives, the line of our culture. They are offered with a prefatory set of questions and considered guesses on the origin, behavior, and destination of story—the chief means by which we became, and stay, human.

*   *   *

The English words *story* and *narrative* come toward us through Greek, Latin, and French from two Proto-Indo-European roots—*weid* and *gno, seeing* and *knowing.* Thus other words related to *story* are *wisdom, vision, wit*; related to *narrative* are *kith, recognition,* and *prognosis.* The etymological messages might be expanded thus—a story is an account of something seen, made visible in the telling. A narrative is an account of something known, especially by the narrator but partially by his audience (their response to total *news* could only be bafflement). Such expansions would seem initially unexceptionable; yet they are not entirely implicit in the definitions given by the dictionary which provides the etymologies (*The American Heritage*)— both words are defined from the point of view of the teller; the audience is considered only as an object to be "interested or amused." Even Webster's Third thinks of the audience only as a passive thing to be cheered, despite the fact that *The Oxford English Dictionary* cites as the earliest use of *story* in English a sentence which is chiefly concerned with audience—"Me schal, leoue sustren, tellen ou theos storie uor hit were to long to writen ham here."[1] (In the following, I use the words *story, narrative*, and *tale* interchangeably because English does, though clear distinctions would be useful.)

Numerous European and American stories of the past fifty or sixty years—say from *Ulysses* onward through Nabokov, Borges, and Beckett to their many disciples in the present American academic tradition— have shared the view of contemporary dictionaries. So far as we can measure the pressures which produced them, they seem to have been more than half reflexive —the story told for the teller's sake (amusement, relief, revenge, reward). Your local bookseller can, while unloading the day's gross of cookbooks and whore's memoirs, tell you the average reader's response to such sealed and guarded stories; and it's my experience that a majority of readers when asked to define *story* will

1. From the *Ancren Riwle*, A.D. 1225.

include themselves as audience in their answer. For years I've asked the question of students as they enter my narrative-writing class, before their views have been pressed on by mine. Here are three responses, thoughtful but typical, from American university students in the immediate past—

> A story is a re-creation of event played out by characters, real or imagined, which unites teller and audience in the recognition of some truth newly remembered or known in a new way.

> A story is a means of creating communion between two people, a teller and a listener, for the purpose of transmitting some knowledge from the teller to the listener.

> A story is a digression from the listener's life offered by the teller as a gift, serving its purpose through their mutual diversion.

A great weight of evidence suggests that an understanding of story as transaction has been basic to the life of narrative as far back as we can see. The very existence of such ancient acts of communication as *Gilgamesh* and the patriarchal cycles of Genesis; the opinions of Plato, Aristotle, Horace, Longinus, the Italian and English Renaissance critics, eighteenth and nineteenth-century European aestheticians—all begin from an assumption that verbal narrative actively seeks an audience. Sir Philip Sidney in 1583 summed the opinion of all theory before the twentieth century—

> [*The poet*] *beginneth not with obscure definitions, which must blur the margent with*

> *interpretations, and load the memory with doubtfulness; but he cometh to you with words set in delightful proportion, either accompanied with, or prepared for, the well-enchanting skill of music; and with a tale forsooth he cometh unto you, with a tale which holdeth children from play, and old men from the chimney corner.*[1]

The vehicle of early narrative (and of virtually all written narrative before Sterne) is simplified in language, rhythm, and structure not because it is "primitive" but because its communication, generally oral, was urgently desired by at least two parties: teller and told. Only as recently as the eighteenth century do we find that what Erich Kahler has called "the inward turn of narrative"[2] results in a trickle of stories which begin to be difficult of access—because they have no desire to be easy or because they lack the ability (among the revelations of Bible narrative is its vast demonstration that the most complex material imaginable may be contained and offered in lucid forms). The floodtide of real obscurity waited another two centuries, for the backwash of romanticism. There may have been difficult ancient narratives which do not survive, and from the beginning of the lyrical impulse there must have been difficult poems. Poets historically have made the

1. Sir Philip Sidney, "The Defense of Poesie" in Allan Gilbert ed., *Literary Criticism: Plato to Dryden* (New York, 1940) p. 427.
2. Erich Kahler, *The Inward Turn of Narrative* (Princeton, 1973) p. 5. "The direction of the interacting development of consciousness and reality is shown . . . to be a progressive internalization of events, an increasing displacement of outer space by what Rilke has called inner space, a stretching of consciousness."

more insistent claim to be god-inspired, therefore subject to tongues or babble; and the lyrical impulse is by nature more directly reflexive than the narrator's. No poet has stated that more fully than the Eskimo hunter Orpingalik—

> Songs are thoughts, sung out with the breath when people are moved by great forces and ordinary speech no longer suffices. Man is moved just like the ice-floe sailing here and there out in the current. His thoughts are driven by a flowing force when he feels joy, when he feels fear, when he feels sorrow. Thoughts can wash over him like a flood, making his breath come in gasps and his heart throb. Something like an abatement in the weather will keep him thawed up. And then it will happen that we, who always think we are small, will feel still smaller. And we will fear to use words. But it will happen that the words we need will come of themselves. When the words we want to use shoot up of themselves—we get a new song.[1]

That would seem a statement congenial to the one great poet who is also an actor in the following pages— David, dancing nude and ecstatically before God in 2 Samuel 6.

It is by no means sure that the chronicler of Saul's and David's reigns, who gives us that picture—the virtual inventor of modern history and biography, five and a half centuries before Herodotus—would have chimed to the sentiment. Nor Homer, who was more nearly a

1. C. M. Bowra, *Primitive Song* (Cleveland, 1962) p. 36.

nineteenth-century novelist than a twentieth-century poet. Wouldn't they have spoken initially of preservation?—preservation of the deeds and thoughts of others for purposes of memory and instruction, the aim which moved Joshua to call for the cairn of stones, "these stones will be a memory to Israel's sons forever" (Joshua 4) or of John in writing his gospel, "These signs have been written so you may believe Jesus is the Messiah, God's son, and so—believing—you may have life in his name" (John 20).

Any such commitment to memory—to narrative simply—is a commitment to free-flowing transaction, to gift and receipt, to the detention however brief of easily bored, forgetful audiences. In fact, despite continuing uncertainty in some linguistic, textual, historical, and theological matters, there are no difficult stories in the Old or New Testaments, none which do not seem quickly visible in the arc of their action to a wide range of human beings and to virtually all veterans of Judeo-Christian culture. In the teeth of sectarian attempts to veil them, convert them into arcana, they remain firmly clear—the core of their meaning plain on their faces, when the faces are scrutinized slowly enough.

—Their meaning as stories, that is (their theological and historical freight, while lightly distributed on the narrative skeleton, can slip past a reader but the story cannot). It is a single meaning, however complex—a meaning evolved over the two thousand years of their composition and the further two thousand of our study; deeply suggestive as I've said, of both the origins of the narrative hunger so basic to man and of the possible future of complex written narrative in industrial societies.

*   *   *

Apparently the oldest words-in-order in the Bible are poems not stories—such fierce songs of triumph as those of Miriam in Exodus 15 and Deborah in Judges 5. The oldest prose stories were set in virtually their present verbal form in about 950 B.C. by one of the greatest of epic writers, anonymous, known to us only as the Yahwist.[1] There is considerable evidence of various sorts however—including the personal experience of anyone reared in a powerful oral-narrative tradition (contemporary American Southerners, for instance, or conservative Jews)—that the stories developed their present narrative armature and perhaps the greater part of their verbal form long before the Yahwist's editing. It seems increasingly likely that the historical figures who stand behind the first of these stories—the three generations of patriarchs: Abraham, Isaac, and Jacob—entered what is now Israel from Mesopotamia in about 1800 B.C. Unless we assume that the patriarchal and Mosaic cycles were invented from whole cloth by the Yahwist or an earlier figure (and no serious contemporary scholar assumes that; on the contrary, movement has been toward a confirmation of the historical reliability of these cycles), then we conclude that the stories are roughly as old as their heroes, surely not more than a generation younger. In that case—and I believe the conclusion to be true—the oldest tale translated here is the account in Genesis 15 of Yahweh's

1. From his insistent use of the proper name of God, *Yahweh*. He is also called J from the German spelling *Jahweh*. The other chief redactor of the older stories here is called the Elohist or E from his use of *Elohim*—"God"—instead of *Yahweh* in pre-Mosaic stories.

covenant with Abraham. Though it is only an episode in the long story of Abraham and the longer story of Israel, it contains the total germ of all those later stories (among the several aspects of narrative perfection in Hebrew and Christian story is the ability to imply all other stories in one).[1]

A god—Yahweh, "I am,"[2] the strongest of a world teeming with gods—so needs one mortal creature that He summons that creature out of his native Mesopotamia; draws him to a new land (the god's home, Canaan); and there in a solemn and mysterious rite "cuts a covenant" with the creature, vowing to pour through his previously sterile loins a race of unique importance to the god, who will inhabit and tend the god's land and worship the god with appropriate rites, despite a period of exile. In a stunned trance the chosen man darkly guesses at the terror of the choice. (It is not however until the end of the exile, five centuries after Abraham, that Yahweh makes explicit to Moses on Sinai—in Exodus 34—"it is terrible what I am about to do with you," a promise whose story resounds through later history and continues.)

If that is a bare summary of the narrative which an

1. A majority of modern students hold that the Pentateuch as we now have it, the first five books of the Hebrew Bible, is the product of four major sources or redactions—a Judean source (J) from about 950 B.C.; a North-Israelite source (E) from about 850; a source exemplified by the book of Deuteronomy (D) from about 650; and a priestly source (P) from the period of Babylonian exile, 550 B.C. and after. The later stories here, of Saul and David, are virtually contemporary with the events they portray, subject to Deuteronomic and Priestly redaction. A good introduction to such problems is Bernhard Anderson's *Understanding the Old Testament* (Englewood Cliffs, 1975).

2. The etymology of *Yahweh* remains a subject of discussion, almost all of which assumes it a form of the Hebrew verb *to be.* The main modern theories are summarized in Anderson, *Understanding the Old Testament,* pp. 53–56.

audience would hear—ancient Hebrew or modern—
what was the narrative heard by the creature himself,
Abram or Abraham? So far as Abraham was the only
human witness to the action, then the version in
Genesis must represent his own understanding, however smoothed and shaped in transmission. Possible
overtones heard by Abraham but not entirely explicit in
Genesis might be phrased as first-person questions—
"Why me? What now? What will any son born under
this condition be?"

Isn't there possibly this question also?—"Is it because He loves me?" Ancient stories of divine passion
for, even infatuation with, a mortal are not rare—Ishtar
and Gilgamesh, Zeus and a multitude, Apollo and
Hyacinth. It is strange however in the prevailing un-
erotic desert air of Genesis to encounter not a Hebrew
parallel to the hijinks of other mythologies (which end
at best in post-coital sadness, at worst in conflagration)
but the startling chance of an origin-in-love, no less
terrifying in the disproportionate capacities of the lovers
but hushed here and ultimately consoling. The same
possibility is implicit in a paired story two thousand
years younger—the annunciation to the Virgin Mary
(Luke 1)—the ancient covenant recut with a girl, an
act also hushed and awful and consoling: *We are loved,
even necessary, though we suffer for it to the point of
cruel death.*

Twenty-six of the thirty stories translated here say
at least that. They affirm the active presence of divine
care and vindication in the lives of God's loyal servants.
Four of the stories—one at the end of each group of
three pairs—say appallingly less: *At times He is absent
or stands, face averted. Creatures are left at the mercy*

of creatures; *they die in agony, no hint of reward.* Yet
even these clots of horror contain reassurance for a
righteous witness. In three of the four stories—the rape
of Dinah, Saul's last night, the killing of Jezebel—those
who suffer are enemies of Yahweh, justly punished.
Only in the sacrifice of Jephthah's daughter is the
victim innocent—*Some wounds, though made by mere
creatures, never heal: we are dreadfully free.*

Stories of violent justice are not rare in the Old
Testament; but even in that harshly-lit world, the
baffled face of a mangled innocent is glimpsed often
enough to confirm the unfrightened breadth of vision
throughout. For all the breadth, however, it is a proof
of the Bible's rejection of *reportorial* wholeness and of
its narrative wisdom that it seems to contain no innocent or virtuous creature dragged protesting toward
painful death—Jephthah's daughter bows to her fate;
Stephen, the first Christian martyr, dies in a vision of
celestial recompense. I call that narrative wisdom since
it acknowledges an absolute essential of the narrative
transaction—it is impossible to tell an audience a story
it does not wish to hear. Perhaps only Jesus—incarnate
God—provides that final story which humans most
dread; if so, it is given without comment and in only
two of the four gospels. Mark, the earliest, records that
Jesus' dying words from the cross were "My God, my
God, why did You forsake me?" followed only by a
great death cry. Matthew agrees. Luke and John provide later resigned, even triumphant speeches.

Any of the hundreds of separate tales in the Old
and New Testaments may be classed under one of
those four types—*We are loved and needed by our
Creator, We suffer but accept our fate, Our enemies*

and God's are rightly punished, and lastly *God is some-times veiled from our sight*. Taken together as a con-tinuing epic of the old landlocked Israel of Abraham and the new universal Israel of Jesus, they form one story which says nothing more. There is nothing more to say, no other story which a wide range of human creatures from all ages will sit still to hear; and those substantial stretches of the Bible which are not mainly story—genealogy, song, law, vision, and essay—only dimly suggest the one other claim a creature can make: *I am here alone, there is no one beyond me, I will soon dissolve*. The Preacher in Ecclesiastes sees that "the righteous man perishes in his righteousness"; Psalm 115 that

The dead do not praise Yah[weh]
    Nor any of those who have gone down to silence.

Such claims—insistent claims of much twentieth-century fiction, drama, and verse—do not, from the point of view of Biblical narrators, constitute a story at all; and in the Bible they are heard only in verse or personal essay, traditionally brief forms. They combine to raise one more or less lyric lament, tolerable to audi-ences only because of brevity, eloquence, and the desire of most men for occasional measured doses of punish-ing fright. To become a story, such a soliloquy of lament would not only have to acquire characters and an action—characters whom an audience could be per-suaded to watch, a major oversight of much modern narrative—but, most importantly, it would need to leave at its end an ultimately consoling effect.

Stories which tell us that the innocent suffer under God's mysterious hand, that our enemies' joints are torn from their sockets, or even that uncontrolled monsters patrol the world (most human beings assume themselves to be monsters, hence the child's fascination with wolves, dinosaurs)—all these can console us in various ways, leave us firmed for our public and private lives. Only the story which declares our total incurable abandonment is repugnant and will not be heard for long. There are no such stories which have won the abiding interest or loyalty of the human species— neither in the Bible nor in the perhaps older surviving tales from Mesopotamia nor in any subsequent literature. Why?

A reflex reply would be *Because such claims are literally intolerable for long.* But the reply of the Yahwist, the Elohist, their oral predecessors, the Christian evangelists, and of most human beings would certainly be *Because they are false.* The all but unanimous testimony of human narrative has embodied, reflected, and sustained the opinion of the species that the figure of man is a sizable piece in the total shape of seen and unseen nature, that the shape itself is partially discernible and nowhere more clearly than in man's own reports on his sightings and soundings—tales, true stories.[1]

Granting that such stories are the oldest known, is there evidence that these carefully formed and transmitted artifacts bear special resemblance to the narratives of early man hundreds of thousands or millions of years previous? Perhaps not evidence but there are at least two kinds of likelihood, though it seems necessary

1. A recent Gallup poll indicates that 34% of all Americans say they have had a decisive experience of conversion to Christianity. 40% of all Americans believe that the Bible is to be interpreted literally, word for word. *Time,* October 4, 1976, p. 75.

to say that the very earliest narratives were probably secular, therefore eventually unsatisfactory.

First, there is the clear fact that narrative, like the other basic needs of the species, supports the literal survival of man by providing him with numerous forms of nurture—the simple companionship of the narrative transaction, the union of teller and told; the narrator's opportunity for exercise of personal skill in telling and its ensuing rewards; the audience's exercise of attention, imagination, powers of deduction; the spiritual support which both parties receive from stories affirming our importance and protection in a perilous world; the transmission to younger listeners of vital knowledge, worldly and unworldly; the narcotic effect of narrative on pain and boredom; and perhaps most importantly, the chance that in the very attempt at narrative transaction something new will surface or be revealed, some sudden floater from the dark unconscious, some message from a god which can only arrive or be told as a tale. Such needs might conceivably have been among the vaguely conscious longings of man before he spoke. It would seem irresistible that the pressure toward such advantages was among the pressures toward speech and therefore narrative. It is difficult, perhaps impossible, to imagine early man, prey as he was to a world of threat, producing stories which did less than arrange the evidence of daily life into sequential, even causal patterns implying order and a certain dependable continuity of life. I am not claiming metaphysical, theological sophistication for proto-narrative, only that certain permanent and orderly cycles of nature might soon have suggested the opposite of chaos (a regular feeding-time still suggests order and safety to mute animals) and thus have resulted in story—the seasons, moon and tide, menstruation, gestation, the rutting of herds, the annual waves of dearth and plenty: story which illuminated present and future by reference to a past both warning and consoling. The more clearly a creature comprehended time and cycle, the stronger his chances for moving with the massive flow of nature, therefore living longer. A skill at true story, as teller or told, made for survival then as now.

Second, once man acquired the complex ability to conceive sequential time, to guess at cause, and to narrate chronologically—*This happened because of that and may happen again*—there would soon have been pressure on teller and told to regress chronologically further and further toward origins, causes, the question *Why? Why did that happen?* It seems inevitable that some of the early answers to *Why?* are preserved in human mythologies. Almost all of those regress to a terminus—creation of world and man by gods. Some of man's remains, older than any known story, point to similar termini—evidences of ritual burial in Europe and the Near East, some sixty thousand years old, imply a hope of afterlife which implies a caring, and storied, god. And to glance again at paleolithic cave painting and the hundreds of exquisitely engraved stones and bones is to confront their radiant numinosity—something transcendent in beast, man, and nature is implored and entreated with delight and reverence.[1]

So while it seems probable that the early eons of

1. Excellent illustrations are available in Marshack, *The Roots of Civilization* and Paolo Graziosi, *Palaeolithic Art* (London, 1960).

narrative were secular—scraps of human hunt, flight, victory; domestic arrangements—the voracious hunger of historical man for origins and causes, operating upon the always ready mass of mystery and the even more basic hunger for solace, would soon arrive at sacred tale: the only perfect story, the story acceptable everywhere as true.

*　　*　　*

That sketch of an evolution omits the force which mythologies posit as crucial—the desire of gods to be known by man, the pressure of transcendent revelation upon creatures who must then narrate or strangle in awe. A contemporary sketch of an unexplored area like the origins of narrative must, in fact, initially omit such a force, if it hopes to reach a wide range of hands.

For the past fifty years, views of the origins of religion and religious story have moved toward polar positions which might crudely be called Freudian and Jungian—the first locating all roots of religious emotion in the structure of the human family, in the great Oedipal ganglion; the second, in the shafts and spelean pools of the collective unconscious. The second position has obviously been more attractive to students naturally inclined to religious emotion and to artists of various sorts, who find the mysterious nature of their own endowments more nearly acknowledged and explained therein. The first position, however—religion as Oedipal tactic—has held the castle of academic critical thought (and medical practice) and continues to do so, though with waning strength against younger generations strongly suspicious of the breadth, depth, and courage of the lines of defense.

I cannot discuss fully here the strengths and weaknesses of those views and of others less prevalent. What I want to do is suggest the beginnings at least of an alternate view, one both older and newer. It is a view which seems to me—and has always seemed, though never more strongly than after these eight years of work—to rise not from theology, dogma, sectarian rite, Oedipal tactic, or world soul but from a particular body of fixed and clearly legible story, unprecedented in the known history of earlier religions and never successfully imitated. Those stories are of course the canonical sacred tales of Jews and Christians. Those tales, and above all the ones gathered here, are their own best witness to the ancient conviction of a sizable portion of the human race that a handful of men over two thousand years on a piece of land hardly larger than the state of North Carolina were brought into intermittent contact with an inhuman power quite beyond that available to comparable tales from other witnesses within our tradition—Assyria, Egypt, Greece.

To examine three tales, however briefly, may clarify some of that witness and suggest further study. I have chosen two reports of divine contact, one of absence and silence.[1]

*　*　*

1. Marshack's speculations on the origins of secular story are careful and interesting—Marshack, *The Roots of Civilization*, pp. 109–123. Evidence of the origin or confirmation of a sacred story is available in John Nance's account of the recent discovery and early study of an isolated stone-age people in the Philippine rain forest—*The Gentle Tasaday* (New York, 1975). Characteristic tales from the ancient Near East are available in J. B. Pritchard ed., *Ancient Near Eastern Texts Relating to the Old Testament* (Princeton, 1969) and Theodor Gaster, *The Oldest Stories in the World* (New York, 1952).

Genesis 32, p. 79 below. Jacob—son of Isaac, grandson of Abraham, the wily thief of his twin-brother Esau's birthright and blessing—had fled to Mesopotamia from his brother's anger and had labored twenty years in bondage to his uncle Laban to earn his beloved Rachel, Laban's daughter. Now, having paid his debt, he is free to return to his homeland—the home of his father's god, "The Fear of Isaac," Yahweh. It is also however the homeland of Esau, whom he cheated twenty years before; and as Jacob reaches the steep-walled ford of Jabbok in the highlands of Gilead east of the Jordan, he receives word that Esau is advancing to meet him with four hundred men. After passing one fearful night in prayer that Yahweh deliver him from Esau, Jacob sends forward a guilt offering—a herd of some six hundred mixed domestic animals. The next night, with still no peaceful word from Esau, Jacob takes his household and belongings across the ford. Then back alone on the far side—to check for stragglers from the flock or in craven terror?—Jacob is assaulted by "some man" who wrestles with him silently and darkly in an uncertain struggle, won only at dawn when the man with a last move dislocates Jacob's hip and engages with him in a reluctant final dialogue. If the story—which must have come from Jacob, its only human witness—ever contained allusions to Jacob's inner questions as the fight proceeded, they are stripped off here in the Yahwist's account. Yet the tense expectation of the last episodes—the approach toward Esau, Jacob's terror—acts upon us as audience to oil the dry leather sinew of the tale with our own best guesses at Jacob's thoughts, the meaning: *Is this Esau, grown even more powerful with years? Or an agent of Esau, sent to murder me by night?* Surely in the early watches, Jacob cannot have known his assailant as Yahweh—the previous night's prayer answered so soon and startlingly. Yet by dawn he has struggled to a kind of recognition. What had seemed "some man" now seems a power with grace to bestow. He has fought with a god whom he still holds down and will not release till he gains a blessing, as he'd gained Esau's from his dying father. And the blessing comes but in strange bent form. The god demands to know his name; he yields it at once, a reckless yielding—his intimate name, the lever to his life, a means to harm him; and a scandal in the land, a swindler's name. With that admission the god gives something more than a ritual blessing—a changed name, a clean slate, forgiveness earned and strength rewarded. The name is *Israel*, God's worthy contestant. Jacob asks the god's name; the god will not say—it should be apparent. With a farewell blessing He departs or disappears. At once Jacob-Israel in the rising light performs the primal human act—the bestowal of name which is also story. He calls the site of his struggle Peniel (or Penuel, both spellings are given)—*God's Face*, "for I saw God face to face and my soul endured." The story we read begins before our eyes in that two-word poem pressed from Jacob in the dawn. The "man" was a god, the God of his father, Yahweh the Fear of Isaac, who had guarded Jacob in his long exile and has now annealed him for the meeting to come with the long-aggrieved Esau. Jacob limps toward the meeting on his injured leg.[1]

1. My reading of the story is indebted to, though in substantial disagreement with, readings in the two distinguished recent commentaries on Genesis—Gerhard von Rad, *Genesis* (Philadelphia, 1961) and E. A. Speiser, *Genesis* (Garden City, 1964).

The story is of a kind which Old Testament criticism calls etiological—told to illuminate the origin of
some fact or practice in tribal history, often one at-
tached to a place made sacred by the action described.
Such a view sees the story of Jacob's struggle as narrative validation of Yahweh's cult center at Penuel on
Jabbok and, less importantly, as explanation of the
name Israel and of the Hebrew dietary ban on the
sciatic muscle; and beyond such a view, criticism barely
goes. Beyond is mystery—speculation, faith, subjective
response. An eagle-eyed modern student like Von Rad
can point out the numerous possible strands of ancient
matter which the Yahwist has woven to his own later
purpose;[1] but a modern reader, religious or not, faced
with the final text, whatever its vicissitudes and earlier
forms, is likely to ask the central question first—*What
does this story ask me to believe?* Either kind of reader
would surely say *It asks me to believe precisely what it
says.*

What it says, in the face of subtilizing comment, is
*All-Powerful God descended in tangible form on a fear-
ful man, fought him all night in hand-to-hand combat,
permitted him to win, then marked him with an injury,
acknowledged his strength in a new grand name,
blessed him, and left him strengthened for his future.*
The text available to us, fixed in about 950 B.C., does
not permit allegorization or spiritualization of the action described. There is no chance of seeing the
struggle as a metaphor of inward event—nightmare,
say. Hebrew sacred narrative roughly contemporary
with the Yahwist—the stories of Saul and David—does
not confront us with such undeniably physical inter-

1. Von Rad, *Genesis*, pp. 314–321.

course between god and man (though the tale of the boy Samuel sees the dim outlines of a visible Yahweh; and later, Elijah can hear His whispering voice). With time and the gathering decay of man, Yahweh had withdrawn such privileges. Whatever the multiple theories of origin (personal memory, manufactured myth, transformed vegetation rite, developed etiology), and despite the nearly one thousand years between the event and the Yahwist's final record, the tale still says that plain thing, a wonder—*Who could have dreamt it? It happened; may again.*

Why should anyone believe it? (millions have, over nearly four millennia). As an object it curiously lacks those irregularities of texture which we expect of true story—the unpredictable instants of visual precision which signal veracity, a recollecting voice. Such instants are common in other Old Testament stories, especially the accounts of Saul, David, and the later monarchs—"They went to bury her and found nothing there but skull and feet and the palms of her hands." And the gospels and Acts swarm with them—Luke says that at the risen Jesus' first appearance to the disciples, he asked for food and "They gave him *part* of a broiled fish" (my italics). Here though, after the careful enumeration of Jacob's household, there is only a lean line tracing the progress of strange encounter. If we try turning the Yahwist's third-person into first, we hear a doubly convincing voice—"When I'd carried them all across, I sent my belongings. Then I was alone and some man wrestled with me there till daybreak"—but in general we must choose among several explanations for the smoothness of surface: the wear of centuries of oral retelling (a process which often results in em-

broidery), some redactor's removal of secular detail
from a sacred story, or the filtering nature of supreme
confidence.

That last seems far the most likely to me. Jacob,
the first narrator, and centuries of subsequent transmit-
ters told a story devoid of small narrative seductions
because they were certain of offering one huge seduc-
tion—*This story is true. I am the man. No one can
doubt me. Why would they, ever? I bring food for
their lives.* The fact that Jacob's tale has been believed
by sizable portions of the human race for thousands of
years, and is still believed and acted on by millions, is
the great reward of his narrative success. No other
narrator, except Abraham, has succeeded longer or
deeper in the first—and final—aim of narrative:
compulsion of belief in an ordered world.

John 21, p. 80. A second tale of revelation,
younger by nearly two thousand years, provides an instructive set of likenesses and contrasts toward a similar
but different narrative end. The Gospel of John records
on a short page the third and final appearance of Jesus,
physically raised from the dead, to seven of his disciples. Contemporary students have not agreed on a
firm date for John or on an identification of its author;
but it would not oversimplify a complex and maybe
insoluble problem to say that in recent decades, a
sizable number of respected students have moved
toward reaffirming the earliest witness (Irenaeus,
Bishop of Lyons, in about A.D. 180) who claimed that
the gospel was written by John, Jesus' beloved disciple,
late in his long life when he was at Ephesus—pre-
sumably before A.D. 100. Even those who argue against
direct or indirect Johannine authorship have steadily

moved toward affirming an early date for the gospel, one within living memory of Jesus.

Jesus was crucified in about A.D. 30. Whoever wrote the Gospel of John—and my own study of the narrative and of its modern critics convinces me that it is solidly based on the aged John's recollections and homilies, recorded by a pupil and subjected to later editing—it was written within, say, sixty years of Jesus' death and the mysteries reflected in the resurrection stories.[1] Sixty years is a short space in human memory, especially short in a society accustomed to oral preservation—the chief fact ignored by the dominant school of modern New Testament scholarship. (As I write this page I am forty-three years old but can summon clear pictorial and auditory memories from forty-one years ago. The oldest lucidly recollecting mind I have met was a woman ninety-nine in 1946—she had been two years old at the deaths of Poe and Chopin.) In a tale such as that in John 21 then there is an extraordinary opportunity to watch the relatively fresh motions of what may be called sacred narrative memory—but *memory* above all, personal recall that might have been corroborated by other witnesses. Let me convert my close translation of the episode into first-person narrative, changing only pronouns and the few other words

1. Students generally see Chapter 21 as an appendix to a book which intended to end with 20. Many however see 21 as a genuinely Johannine story, appended later as too valuable to lose. The account of the chapter in Raymond Brown, *The Gospel According to John*, vol. II (Garden City, 1970) both summarizes recent study and sees in the chapter a conflation of two or more differing tales. Despite Brown's meticulous intelligence, I go on seeing only one tale in 21—an aged worn memory but seamless all the same.

necessary to flush the beloved disciple from the near-hiding he has imposed on himself throughout his book.

> *Another time Jesus showed himself to us by the Sea of Tiberias—showed himself this way.*
>
> *Simon Peter was there with Thomas whom we called "Twin," Nathanael from Cana in Galilee, my brother James and I, and two more of Jesus' disciples. Simon Peter said to us "I'm going out fishing."*
>
> *We said "We're coming with you." So we went out and got in the boat. But all night we caught nothing.*
>
> *Then when day broke Jesus stood on the shore though none of us knew it was Jesus.*
>
> *He called to us "Boys, anything to eat?"*
>
> *We said "No."*
>
> *So he said to us "Cast the net to starboard—you'll find them."*
>
> *We cast and the crowd of fish was so big we couldn't haul it.*
>
> *Then I said to Peter "It's the Lord."*
>
> *When Peter heard that, he cinched up his shirt—under it he was naked—and threw himself into the sea.*
>
> *We others came on in the little boat towing the net of fish—we were only a hundred yards or so from land—and when we landed we saw a charcoal fire laid with fish laid on it and bread.*
>
> *Jesus said to us "Bring some of the fish you caught."*

> *So Peter got up and hauled in the net full*
> *of big fish—a hundred and fifty-three—and*
> *with all the number still the net held.*
>
> *Jesus said "Come eat breakfast."*
>
> *Not one of us dared ask "Who are you?"*
> *We knew it was the Lord.*
>
> *Jesus came over, took the bread and gave*
> *it to us. Also the fish.*
>
> *This was the third time Jesus showed him-*
> *self to us after being raised from the dead.*

To perform that neat transformation is not necessarily to demonstrate the existence of a nearly identical first-person original. Oral tales, since they seldom deal in internal emotion (thought, doubt, soliloquy), lend themselves more readily to interchangeable viewpoints than do dense, written tales. Any practiced novelist, however, knows that when an entire third-person narrative can be mechanically converted into natural first-person then there is likely to be a strong personal vision and voice beneath the strategies of distance and anonymity.

In the case of John 21, the voice resembles that of Genesis 32 so far as they both speak of intimate, even physical—but all the more mysterious—contact with what was taken at once and later as divine energy. John, near as he is to the contact, offers the convincing knotty texture which was largely missing in Jacob's struggle—Jesus' call to them as "boys" (plural of the Greek *paidion*, diminutive of *pais*, boy); the detail of Peter's dress (I've accepted Raymond Brown's view that Peter *cinches up* not *puts on* his shirt, revealing both his near-hysteria and his nudity); the professional fishermen's practicality in coming on slowly with the catch as contrasted to Peter's characteristic abandon; the odd note that "Peter got up and hauled in the net" (a further hint that the narrator is witnessing a pictorial memory but has neglected to communicate all his vision—where did Peter get up from: a bow at Jesus' feet or breathless prostration in the shallows?); the precise count of fish (in which centuries of commentators have strained for symbolism, without convincing result); and the unembroidered gravity of the plain but sacramental breakfast.

Comparison with a parallel incident in early uncanonical Christian literature would provide an interesting check on the quality of memorial vision in John. The promising fragmentary apocryphal *Gospel of Peter* (about A.D. 150) breaks off just as it begins to parallel John 21—

> *Now it was the last day of unleavened bread and many went away and repaired to their homes, since the feast was at an end. But we, the twelve disciples of the Lord, wept and mourned, and each one, very grieved for what had come to pass, went to his own home. But I, Simon Peter, and my brother Andrew took our nets and went to the sea. And there was with us Levi, the son of Alphaeus, whom the Lord. . . .*[1]

But the apocryphal *Acts of Pilate* (about fourth century) puts into the mouth of Joseph of Arimathea an

1. Edgar Hennecke, *New Testament Apocrypha*, Wilhelm Schneemelcher ed. and R. McL. Wilson trans. (Philadelphia, 1963) I, p. 187.

extended first-person account of a resurrection appearance—

> *On the day of preparation about the tenth hour you shut me in, and I remained the whole Sabbath. And at midnight as I stood and prayed, the house where you shut me in was raised up by the four corners, and I saw as it were a lightning flash in my eyes. Full of fear I fell to the ground. And someone took me by the hand and raised me up from the place where I had fallen, and something moist like water flowed from my head to my feet, and the smell of fragrant oil reached my nostrils. And he wiped my face and kissed me and said to me: Do not fear, Joseph. Open your eyes and see who it is who speaks with you. I looked up and saw Jesus. Trembling, I thought it was a phantom, and I said the commandments. And he said them with me. Now as you well know, a phantom immediately flees if it meets anyone and hears the commandments. And when I saw that he said them with me, I said to him: Rabbi Elijah! He said: I am not Elijah. And I said to him: Who are you, Lord? He replied: I am Jesus, whose body you asked for from Pilate, whom you clothed in clean linen, on whose face you placed a cloth, and whom you placed in your new cave, and you rolled a great stone to the door of the cave. And I asked him who spoke to me: Show me the place where I laid you. And he took me and showed me the*

*place where I laid him. And the linen cloth
lay there, and the cloth that was upon his face.
Then I recognized that it was Jesus. And he
took me by the hand and placed me in the
middle of my house, with the doors shut, and
led me to my bed and said to me: Peace be
with you! Then he kissed me and said to me:
Do not go out of your house for forty days.
For see, I go to my brethren in Galilee.*[1]

Despite the physical extravagance of the passage, it
stands as perhaps the least fanciful of the numerous
surviving uncanonical tales of the resurrection. There is
of course the possibility that the author of John 21 was
simply a narrator of greater restraint and skill than
those responsible for uncanonical tales; but there are
important questions which such a comparison raises,
not only for New Testament scholarship and Christian
faith but for the metaphysics of narrative—does
canonical (approved, acceptable) in the matter of
Hebrew and Christian sacred texts finally mean *credible*?
Are Matthew, Mark, Luke, and John our only
canonical stories of the life of Jesus because they are
immediately perceptible as the best stories—the most
credible in their consolations, the least manipulative in
their fancies and designs upon us? Finally, the resurrection
stories of the canonical gospels, especially those
translated here, raise in ultimate form the question all
narrative enterprise must face—how long will audiences
accept, and to what uses can they put, any narration
which is not, first, a reliable report? It is clear that large
numbers will wait through fantastic, even terrifying,

1. Hennecke, *New Testament Apocrypha* I, p. 466.

tales and return to them for years—provided they are labeled *false*. What if a narrator claims urgent truth, truth to bend our lives, but offers a lie?

Such a voice as that in John's resurrection tales or in Luke's is either reporting truly or lying brilliantly for political purpose, though we must consider the slim possibility that John and Luke were defrauded by events explicable in terms other than those provided them. I, like millions, am convinced and have always been by the stories themselves—their narrative perfection, the speed and economy with which they offer all the heart's last craving in shapes as credible as any friend's tale of a morning walk. And despite its greater age, its dimmer lines, I also yield to the tale of Jacob's struggle—helpless belief. If John and Luke tell me of acts more urgent for my own daily life, as a veteran of Christian parents and culture, that was their huge luck as witnesses and heirs of quiet events at the core of light. From the point of view of human need, the tale of Jacob at Penuel is as useful, in matter and manner. Both the Yahwist and John are treading the narrow white ridge of the summit of story in dazzling view of the perfect tale men dream and crave, yet not dazzled by it—watchful and capable in their certain joy to have seen the true tale and *lasted* as competent witnesses, actual angels to blinder men: *We are treasured; the wheel of the sky knows of us, turns to yield us light.* Fresh names, clean starts; a palpable god; bread, also fish.

1 *Samuel* 28, p. 105. The darker tales here, and in all sacred stories, are the gorges implicit in such bright peaks; and the extended account of Yahweh's abandonment of Saul, His first anointed king, is among the

most carefully shaped and longest admired of all Biblical reports. The action described—eve of the battle at Gilboa in which Saul and his three sons died—occurred in about 1000 B.C. In the opinion of an important student, our tale of Saul and the witch at Endor derives from tradition local to Endor, perhaps even to the witch's own house, and is a basically untouched contemporary account.[1] Yet unless we assume that the witch herself transmitted the tale (not an impossibility, considering the sympathetic light in which she appears) or that it is invented, we are forced to conclude that the narrative bones of the present tale originated in the memory of at least one of the two slave witnesses—perhaps Philistines themselves; in any case, hardly worshippers of Yahweh. If that is the origin—a first-hand account of visible and audible events from a memorable night—then we also conclude that someone intervened later with an ear for Yahweh's dreadful silence and with a human voice for tragic comprehension and pity. Saul had once, eager for battle, usurped Samuel's priestly rites; later he had disobeyed Yahweh's specific command to exterminate the Amalekites; Yahweh had turned His face. The effects of the abandonment had gathered slowly—Saul's recurrent attacks of profound depression; Samuel's enmity; the rise (and Samuel's anointing) of David, Saul's protégé-turned-nemesis; and at last Yahweh's unrelenting silence as the Philistines wait for dawn by their campfires. Yet the silence does relent, in an awful way. Though Saul has purged the country of unorthodox channels to divine or demonic energy—witches and

1. Hans Wilhelm Hertzberg, *I & II Samuel* (Philadelphia, 1964) p. 217.

wizards—a chance survives at Endor: one possessed woman. He and two slaves approach her disguised; and faced with the hope of consulting any spirit, Saul can only ask for Samuel, his prophet-anointer and the hectoring bane of his kingship. He had last seen Samuel alive at Gilgal when, before the ark of Yahweh, Samuel hacked to pieces Agag, king of the Amalekites, whom Saul had spared. The witch's power works and Samuel rises reluctantly from the dead to hear Saul's plea—"I have called you to tell me what I must do." The voice which, living, had poured a stream of advice to Saul can now only echo the silence of God—*You have disobeyed the Force that will not bear disobeying; "Tomorrow you and your sons shall be with me."* The speech is true; Saul is poleaxed by it. The spirit vanishes; only the woman, the hunted frightened witch, and Saul's two slaves remain to console him with the last of helps—food: hastily butchered veal and flatcakes. He has been consigned to men—Yahweh's last worst punishment—and even men fail him. Tomorrow in the battle the Philistines will miss him; and when he sees defeat and orders his armor-bearer to dispatch him on the field, the armor-bearer will refuse.[1] Saul must even kill himself. Swathed in a human tenderness as rare as water in the fierce hills, Saul's end says the thing all God's desertions say—*Stories of man, unassisted man, are the only tragedies: ignorance, waste, savagery of heart.*

The one scene comparable for situation and tenderness in western literature—that Plutarchan moment in *Antony and Cleopatra* (IV, iii) when Antony's god

1. Was the armor-bearer one of Saul's two companions at Endor?

deserts him on the eve of his own last battle—does not approach the force and terror of the muffled night at Endor:

MUSIC OF THE HOBOYS IS UNDER THE STAGE.

2ND SOLDIER.   *Peace, what noise?*

1ST SOLDIER.   *List, list!*

2ND SOLDIER.   *Hark!*

1ST SOLDIER.   *Music i' th' air.*

3RD SOLDIER.   *Under the earth.*

4TH SOLDIER.   *It signs well, does it not?*

3RD SOLDIER.   *No.*

1ST SOLDIER.   *Peace, I say.*
What should this mean?

2ND SOLDIER.   *'Tis the god Hercules, whom Antony lov'd,*
Now leaves him.

1ST SOLDIER.   *Walk; let's see if other watch-men*
Do hear what we do.

*   *   *

To claim that those tales stand a strong chance of being true in a literal sense—that they offer us eye-witness reports of events theoretically visible to eyes other than the participants', events recordable on tape and film if such means had been available—is not only to risk a simplicity of comprehension bordering on the simpletonian but also to turn one's face on two centuries of investigation and speculation by hundreds of students of rite, myth, cultural evolution, comparative religions, the psychopathology of the sacred, and multiple schools of textual study of the Old and New Testaments.

The volume of such studies is now so great, and continuing, that a single reader can barely hope to encompass and synthesize. Weston La Barre has come as near as anyone.[1] It was in his classes at Duke twenty-three years ago that I began my own patrols through the field—first the labyrinths of Tylor and Frazer, then on without system but with undiminished appetite to the present: all, I think, in a long attempt to disprove to myself the preposterous claim of the earliest stories I had known and loved; an attempt to assault the bases of my life.

The attempt has failed till now at least—this book records that—so I do make the claim or one form of it. A number of the theophanies in the Old and New Testaments give emphatic narrative evidence of claiming to be eyewitness reports of external events (another group make no such claim—such accounts as Exodus 3, 1 Samuel 3, and Luke 1 seem *as narratives* to permit our understanding them as metaphors of internal event; the choice between claims is one more gauntlet flung down to mother-wit). They bear their validation in the narrative bones, bones of the visible actions they describe, and in the reckless bravery on their cloudless faces. They well understand that they give us one choice—if we call them untrue, we must call them insane. They are plainly not deceitful; and I plainly call them true, in some awareness of the range of objections.

I would like to explore three things at greater

1. Weston La Barre, *The Ghost Dance: Origins of Religion* (New York, 1970). La Barre's text and notes provide an excellent guide to the literature; and the fact that I deeply disagree with his views on the sources of religion does not prevent gratitude for the bracing shock he administered to childhood predilections.

length. First, the objections themselves and the pressure of motives behind them. Second, the narrative strategies of the tales as artifacts stunningly successful over time and place in their own first aims, and in aims accreted to them through millennia, and rich with lessons for recent generations of narrators oddly bent on repelling or petrifying a large waiting audience (especially interesting would be the question of how they carry for so many readers a reportorial conviction that sets them firmly apart from such seductive, partially satisfying but clearly fictional narratives as those of Stendhal, Flaubert, Tolstoy, Chekhov). Third, the psychic components of my long fascination with these few stories, my propensity to believe them.

I hope to do all three at another time—each is perhaps a separate book—but my purpose here was to preface a group of translated stories with the larger questions they have raised for me and to offer the lot in the hope of pointing new readers to an old and patient source of pleasure, instruction, and nourishment—a source of which their recent training has deprived them. I have also hoped to provide older readers with fresh and provoking but faithful tracings of deep-cut cornerstones worn smooth in their minds; and lastly, to share with colleagues in the craft of narrative a chance for contemplation of what has seemed, in our civilization, both the source and end of story itself.

Human narrative, through all its visible length, gives emphatic signs of arising from the profoundest need of one fragile species. Sacred story is the perfect answer given by the world to the hunger of that species for true consolation. The fact that we hunger has not precluded food.

A NOTE ON
TRANSLATION
AND SELECTION

I HAVE said that I began these versions with no
knowledge of Hebrew beyond an ability to recognize
the Tetragrammaton, God's name, and with almost no
Greek. I worked from literal interlinear versions with
steady reference to an important text which I could
read—Jerome's Latin Vulgate, a translation which is
not only the Bible of the Roman Church but is
virtually a primary text itself, based on manuscripts and
translations available to Jerome in the third and fourth
centuries but now lost.[1] And since the Bible is by far
the most microscopically examined and described text
in the history of literature, I consulted from the first
relevant modern commentaries on all the stories (it is

1. George Ricker Berry, *Interlinear Hebrew-English Old
Testament* [*Genesis-Exodus*] (Grand Rapids, 1970). Joseph
Magil, *The Englishman's Hebrew-English Old Testament* [*Gene-
sis-2 Samuel*] (Grand Rapids, 1974). Joseph Bryant Rotherham,
The Emphasized Bible (Grand Rapids, 1971), a literal but not
interlinear version. George Ricker Berry, *The Interlinear Literal
Translation of the Greek New Testament* (Grand Rapids, 1971).
Alfred Marshall, *The Interlinear Greek-English New Testament*
(Grand Rapids, 1972). Robert Weber ed., *Biblia Sacra Iuxta
Vulgatam Versionem*, I-II (Stuttgart, 1969).

possible to find elaborate linguistic notes to virtually every word in them).[1] Then as my interest whetted and a sequence of stories seemed desirable, I faced the question of whether to study Hebrew and Greek. Various jobs made unlikely the acquisition of real skill in both; and since the gospels had always provided the most personally urgent of the texts, I began to add to my college-fraternity Greek. I therefore reached the end of the sequence—and revised all the others—with some ability to deal with the Koiné Greek New Testament, sufficient when all else failed to roam comfortably in the best modern New Testament lexicon and to study comparative textual editions.[2]

My New Testament versions then can claim direct if imperfect contact with the best available editions of the original; those from the Old Testament are based upon the best literal English versions and the Vulgate. The method is not ideal, though it is one widely used

1. The previously cited commentaries on Genesis by Von Rad and Speiser were invaluable as was Hertzberg's *I & II Samuel*, Brown's *John*, and Martin Noth's *Exodus* (Philadelphia, 1962). A model of New Testament commentary—and literary wisdom—is found in Vincent Taylor's *The Gospel According to Mark* (New York, 1969). Other commentaries—old and new, too numerous to mention—were consulted on individual passages; but my chief helps were those listed. Among numerous good introductions to the New Testament, an especially lucid example is W. D. Davies' *Invitation to the New Testament* (Garden City, 1969).

2. Walter Bauer, *A Greek-English Lexicon of the New Testament and Other Early Christian Literature*, W. F. Arndt and F. W. Gingrich eds. and trans. (Chicago, 1974). The Old Testament versions are based on the Masoretic text as occasionally amended by my various guides (I have often rejected emendations, on instinct). The New Testament versions rest, with very few changes, on the standard modern text—Kurt Aland, Matthew Black, Bruce Metzger, and Allen Wikgren, *The Greek New Testament* (London, 1966).

in varying ways for centuries—one which has produced some memorable, occasionally uncanny results. Though Luther possessed decent Hebrew and better Greek, his German Bible relies on Greek and Latin and earlier German translations; and the King James itself, while adept in Hebrew and Greek as understood in its time, relies on the Vulgate and other Latin versions, on continental vernacular versions, and so heavily on earlier English versions by Tyndale, Coverdale, and the Bibles of Geneva and Rheims as to be virtually a collage made from them. Chapman's Homer, Pope's Homer, Fitzgerald's *Rubaiyat,* and various admired translations by Pound, Auden, Spender, and Robert Lowell are among many based on intermediate vernacular versions of inaccessible originals.

My second hope as a translator is that twenty-one years of work as a narrator of human encounters with the sacred—and more than forty years as native and resident of a culture steeped in *told* story—will add to my versions a degree of that intuitive possession of and by an original which distinguishes those earlier examples (the first hope is not to have misrepresented such vital matter).

When I say that I have worked with the help of literal translations toward what I believe to be as literal a *reading* text as exists in modern English, then the large question of literalness arises—what is a literal translation? is it possible or desirable?

There are extremes of literalness which result in language usable only by students, the schoolboy's dream of a pony to Caesar or Vergil. An excellent example of extreme literalness is this version of a passage from Mark 5—

*And they are coming into the house of the
chief of the synagogue, and He is beholding
a tumult, and they are lamenting much and
screaming. And entering, He is saying to them,
"Why are you making a tumult and lamenting? The little girl did not die, but is drows-
ing." And they ridiculed Him. Yet He,
ejecting them all, is taking along the father
of the little girl and the mother and those
with Him, and He is going in where the little
girl was lying. And, holding the hand of the
little girl, He is saying to her, "Talitha,
coumi!" (which is, being construed, "Maiden,
I am saying to you, rouse!"). And straightway
the maiden rose and walked about, for she was
about twelve years old.*[1]

That is the result of a self-consistent effort to convert,
in order, one word of Greek into one word of English
(always into the same word) and to convey all tenses;
and in its uncouthness, it is truer to its original and
conveys a more compelling experience than many
smoother attempts—literal travesties.

Here is another version which attempts word-for-
word in order, tenses conveyed, but without commitment to consistent translation of each Greek word—

*And they come into the house of the syna-
gogue chief, and he sees an uproar, and [men]
weeping and crying aloud much, and entering
he says to them: Why make ye an uproar and*

1. *Concordant Literal New Testament* (Saugus, 1966)
pp. 100–101. I cannot reproduce the complex typographical
system by which this version further indicates linguistic subtleties
of the original.

*weep? the child did not die but sleeps. And
they ridiculed him. But he putting out all
takes the father of the child and the mother
and the [ones] with him, and goes in where
was the child. And taking hold of the hand
of the child he says to her: Talitha koum,
which is being interpreted: Maid, to thee I say,
arise. And immediately rose up the maid and
walked; for she was of years twelve.*[1]

Here is the King James of 1611—

*And he cometh to the house of the ruler of
the Synagogue, and seeth the tumult, and
them that wept and wailed greatly. And when
he was come in, he saith unto them. Why
make ye this ado, and weep? the damsel is not
dead, but sleepeth. And they laughed him to
scorn: But when he had put them all out, he
taketh the father and the mother of the
damsel, and them that were with him, and
entereth in where the damsel was lying. And
he took the damsel by the hand, and said unto
her, Talitha cumi; which is, being interpreted,
Damsel (I say unto thee) Arise. And straightway the damsel arose, and walked, for she was
of the age of twelve years.*

And the New English Bible as revised in 1970—

*They came to the president's house, where he
found a great commotion, with loud crying*

1. Marshall, *The Interlinear Greek-English New Testament*, pp. 158–159.

*and wailing. So he went in and said to them,
'Why this crying and commotion? The child
is not dead: she is asleep'; and they only
laughed at him. But after turning all the
others out, he took the child's father and
mother and his own companions and went in
where the child was lying. Then, taking hold
of her hand, he said to her, 'Talitha cum',
which means, 'Get up, my child.' Immediately
the girl got up and walked about—she was
twelve years old.*

If we take the second version as a model of
modern interlinear-literal, then we can see that the
King James is hewing to its loosely held, sanely applied
principle of literalness and that it attempts to give
original tenses. The New English Bible is clearly freer,
though closer than it often is. Both conceal Mark's vivid
and tender distinction between *paidion* (child) which
the narrative employs up to the healing and *korasion*
(little girl) which renders the Aramaic Jesus uses in the
great moment and which the narrative then echoes—
"Grasping the child's hand he said to her *'Talitha
koum'* which is translated 'Little girl, I tell you rise.' At
once the little girl stood and walked round." But it is in
an apparently smaller matter that the New English
Bible reveals its characteristic disloyalty, one of which
the King James is almost never guilty. In the first sentence of the passage, Mark says that Jesus *sees*
(*theorei*) an uproar. The first three versions preserve
the verb; the New English Bible says he *found*. Bauer
gives *perceive, see* as the first meaning and *notice, ob-
serve, find* as the second; but Mark implies a sensory

experience in Jesus—he enters and *sees*; then he responds.

The Old and New Testaments are unremittingly physical in their articulation, like most other sane human narrations—action follows and is generally caused by sensory perception of some previous action. Failure to convey that reality is failure to tell the story, failure to confront and recreate (in a language like English, equally capable of the reality) the embarrassing and demanding corporeality of the original.

It is a failure endemic to most contemporary translations. The Jerusalem Bible and J. B. Phillips say "Jesus noticed." E. V. Rieu says "he was faced by a disorderly scene." Ronald Knox says "he found" (violating the plain first sense of his prime text, the Vulgate, which has *videt*).[1] Of widely used recent versions, only the Revised Standard preserves *saw*.

A list of similar failures would be long—there are several on almost any page—but one more example will serve. In Exodus 4 when Yahweh tells Moses to return to Egypt and demand his people's freedom from Pharaoh, Moses replies that he is not an appropriate messenger. Berry's literal translation is "O Lord, not a man of words [am] I, both from yesterday and from the third day, and since thy speaking unto thy servant; for heavy of mouth and heavy of tongue [am] I." But Yahweh insists, "And now go, and I will be with thy mouth, and will teach thee what thou shalt speak."[2]

1. *The Jerusalem Bible* (Garden City, 1966). J. B. Phillips trans., *The Gospels* (New York, 1959). E. V. Rieu trans., *The Four Gospels* (Harmondsworth, 1958). Ronald Knox trans., *The Holy Bible* (London, 1961).

2. Berry, *Interlinear Hebrew-English Old Testament*, pp. 231–232.

King James preserves the physical claustrophobia implicit in the Hebrew image—"I will be with thy mouth"—and the Revised Standard follows. But Knox again violates both Hebrew and his Latin original (*ego ero in ore tuo*) by giving "I will speak with thy mouth"; and the New English collapses into its usual explanation and abstract commonness, "I will help your speech and tell you what to say."

What the abstractionists are saying is plain—"The original of course employed its resources of limited vocabulary and primitive imagery to the limit, but what we must tell you is what they *meant* to say." In its fidelity not to what was meant but to what was actually seen and said (and *therefore* meant), the King James and its English predecessors achieved their triumph— for close study will show that the qualities of vision, narrative vigor, style, and rhythm which have made King James not only the most influential work in our literature but unshakably the Bible for three centuries of believers are not the product of supreme literary skill in the translators or of the benevolent *Zeitgeist* of Elizabethan-Jacobean England but of loyalty to a simple principle. In the general assumption that almost every word of a narrative or lyric original may be transmuted, however mysteriously, into a close visual equivalent in the vernacular, the King James awarded itself an enduring distinction—a continuous poetry rooted in and blossoming from our only means of knowledge: the human body and its fragile organs.

That is not to claim that the King James is any longer a satisfactory translation of the originals, as we now have them. The Hebrew and Greek texts available in seventeenth-century England were sadly inaccurate; and hundreds of matters (linguistic, rhythmic, historical) now comprehended or clarified were dark then—especially the Koiné Greek of the New Testament, so imperfectly understood by scholars trained in classical Greek and lacking the mass of papyrus and scroll unearthed in the nineteenth and twentieth centuries. The Revised Standard, in its redaction of King James, is the closest contemporary approach to a satisfactory conversion of the original in its own terms of bone and sinew, though in their moments of independence the translators reveal a middling command of plain English. An adequate attempt on the whole, in its range of genres and effects, would require the service not only of the linguists, textual critics, and theologians who labored on the Revised Standard, the New English, and the Jerusalem versions but of writers by nature and experience, men and women who would not attempt to apply an external beauty to originals which are often rough but who might catch the tones of ancient voices, their indelible copies of sightings of a power content to approach us in our human shape, the figure He honored enough to create.

*   *   *

The passages below make no effort at representing the range of the original. Laws, prophets, psalms, and the wisdom literature of the Old Testament are missing; and the polemics and epistles of the New. It might even be wondered why, in a collection which begins as a study of the origins of human narrative, stories so relatively new as those in the New Testament should be set beside the Old.[1] I've implied the answer—personal motives aside, it is clear that in the gospels and Acts, we have a chance unique in our civilization for observing the rise and recording of primal sacred tales in close proximity to the events which generated them. They provide us also with complex and delicate equipment for gauging the qualities of historicity and fabulation—of need and honesty—in older tales. What is here is what I believe to be the core of sacred *story*— God's appearances to man, His withdrawals from him: presences and absences, our deepest hope and terror. The passages are organized in a way that may seem factitious to the reader but was important to me as I worked—an introductory Hebrew poem in the voice of God; four groups of presences or theophanies, arranged by related pairs from Old and New Testaments, each followed by an absence; a long story from the Old Testament, portraying both presence and absence; a parallel long story from the New; and a final New Testament poem in the voice of God.

I have already implied my procedure—given the declared limitations, I attempt to convert the words of an original in their full sensory implications into the

1. Precise dating of the gospels and Acts is still a matter of such passionate dispute as to make a summary note impossible. It would, however, be accurate to say that many students—perhaps a majority—believe Mark to be the oldest gospel, composed about A.D. 65, some thirty-five years after Jesus' death. Matthew and Luke (who also claims to be author of Acts) are believed to rely on Mark, among other sources, and to follow him by from ten to twenty years. John is the subject of especially heavy debate; but as I have indicated, steady movement seems to be in the direction of dating it, like the other gospels, within the first generation of those who knew Jesus—before A.D. 100.

strict minimum of appropriate English words, preserving the original order of word-therefore-vision whenever possible. I debated preserving the often startlingly effective shifts of tense, especially the gospels' abrupt leaps from past to present and back—

> At once going up out of the water he saw the
> sky being torn open and the Spirit like a dove
> descending to him. There was a voice out of
> the sky "You are My son, the loved one. In
> you I have delighted." And at once the Spirit
> drives him into the desert. . . .
>
> (Mark 1, my emphasis)—

but in the end, I found strict fidelity to be unnerving to readers of contemporary written English and have fallen back on the imposed consistency of other modern versions—universal past tenses: some loss, some gain.

There were smaller possible fidelities which I abandoned for similar reasons. Accustomed to the King James, we think of the Bible as a string of short clauses bound at frequent intervals by the word *and*. Indeed, the omnipresent *and* has been the greatest single influence of the King James on the idea of eloquence in subsequent English. Hebrew and Greek originals are more than amply provided with their respective connective particles *wāw* and *kai*; but students now contend that, in either language, the particle bore a number of narrative connotations not suggested by an invariable *and*—connotations such as *then, while, however*, and *namely*. Further, since neither language employed systematic punctuation, the particles frequently indicated no more than the start of a new sentence. I have trimmed my _ands_ and have translated the particle as _then_ only when a narrative progression demanded notice. In my version of the longer story of Joseph, I have converted the frequent Hebrew _land of Egypt / land of Canaan_ into the less cumbersome _Egypt_ and _Canaan_; I have often simplified the construction _he spoke to his brother, saying_ to _he said to his brother._ Elsewhere I have occasionally omitted insistent stage-directions in dialogue—"he said _to them_"—and at the beginning of a story I have sometimes added a word for narrative clarity—"Eli _the priest_"—or changed a pronoun to the relevant name; and throughout I have given the reader a slightly illegitimate advantage in the thicket of unspecified Hebrew pronouns by capitalizing the pronouns referring to Yahweh, though not those referring to the earthly Jesus.

Otherwise, I have worked at what I hope is a sane consistency. I preserve the proper name of God wherever it is given. The best evidence makes virtually certain that the Hebrew Tetragrammaton _YHWH_ was pronounced _Yahweh_ (most versions, including the King James, give the name as _the Lord_, a translation of the periphrastic Hebrew _Adonai_; or they perpetuate the incorrect medieval transliteration _Jehovah_). And while I am not committed to the crippling consistency of always translating a given Hebrew or Greek word by the same English word, I work toward a sense of the strictly limited vocabularies of the originals. Modern versions err badly in assuming that a given English word may not convey as many shades of meaning as one in Hebrew or Greek, and they therefore employ a needlessly varied and misleading array of words (the

Hebrew Old Testament employs only about eight thousand words, of which two thousand appear only once; Shakespeare employs about twenty-one thousand). For example, I am consistent, I think, in English equivalents for the three Greek verbs which Mark continually employs to describe the world's responses to Jesus—*amazed, astonished, stunned.* I have done the same with his frequent and characteristic *euthus, at once,* and with the most striking characteristic of Jesus' personal diction—his apparently unique use of *Amen* to preface a solemn statement (translated V*erily* in the King James). On the other hand, I vary my rendering of the Hebrew and Greek possessive, which is generally the *so-and-so of so-and-so,* by employing the English *'s* construction.

I have mentioned the absence of punctuation from the originals. I attempted stripping all such marks from my versions only to find the result again unnerving and misleading. I compromise, providing English punctuation where confusion might occur. I paragraph to indicate changes of speaker and changes of actor, in the hope of conveying visually an actual physical isolation of actors which the narrative forces upon them. The line and movement of the tales are obscured by the dense typography of modern versions, as they are by chapter and verse division (which were no part of the originals, our present system being introduced into both Testaments by Robert Estienne in his folio French Bible of 1553). Since these versions are not primarily intended for scholars, I omit verse numbers. Italic passages in gospel stories are quotations from or close allusions to the Old Testament.

In short, I have aimed for the most literal reading

versions possible in modern English—as limited in range and color of word and image as their originals require them to be and as clear, but not more so. (By the time the archaic diction of the oral tales of the Pentateuch was transcribed, it cannot have made smooth—or always comprehensible—reading for many Jews, if any; and among Christian evangelists, only Luke used Greek with idiomatic fluency. Mark, Matthew, and John wrote with vigor and intensity but hardly with invariable elegance, syntactical lucidity, or naturalness. The pursuit of naturalness, which impels many recent translations of the Bible, assumes that a twentieth-century student can acquire a perfect ear for the impressions which ancient stories—precise locutions, tones, sounds—would have made upon original audiences and that he can then reproduce those impressions with some accuracy upon readers of contemporary Anglo-American English. However skilled the linguist, the assumption has proved unverifiable and has frequently produced distortions of architecture and atmosphere nearly fatal to successful narrative transaction.) The versions here hope at least to avoid treacherous smoothness and to yield some contact, however muffled, with the grain of that old life, startling in its ribbed strength and dangerous still. None of my hopes has obscured for long, though, the fact which chastens any such job—that "all translations . . . are but arrested pursuits of the given source"[1] which flees ahead, blood and life intact, into newer and newer nets of men.

1. Speiser, *Genesis*, p. lxxiv.

THE STORIES

Yahweh shall judge His people and shall have mercy on His slaves. When He sees their strength is vanished—that there is no savior, bound or free—then He shall say

> "Where are their gods?—
> Rock where they hid,
> Who ate fat of sacrifice,
> Drank poured wine?
> Let them stand and help you.
> Let them be your shelter.
> See now that I,
> I am He.
> No gods with Me.
> I kill and I raise,
> I hurt and I heal.
> No flight from My hand.
> I raise My hand to sky
> And swear
>> 'As I live forever—
>> When I whet lightning of my sword
>> And My hand seize vengeance,
>> I will pay My foes,
>> Hurt My haters.
>> I will make My arrows
>> Drunk with blood,
>> My sword swill flesh,
>> Blood of the slain

> And prisoners,
> The heads of their princes.' "

Shout joy, O nations. He avenges the blood of His slaves, pays His foes, is good to the ground of his people.

The word of Yahweh came in vision to Abram saying "No fear, Abram. I am a shield for you. Your reward shall be huge."

Abram said "O Lord Yahweh, what can You give me since I go on childless and the heir to my house is Dammesek Eliezer?" And Abram said "Look, You have given no seed and—look—a man of my house will inherit from me."

Look, the word of Yahweh saying "This one shall not inherit from you but he who shall go out from your own body, he shall inherit from you." He took him out and said "See the sky now and count the stars if you can count them." He said to him "So your seed shall be."

He trusted Yahweh.

So He laid it to his goodness and said to him "I am Yahweh who brought you out from Ur of the Chaldees to give you this land to own."

He said "O Lord Yahweh, how shall I know that I am to own it?"

He said to him "Bring Me a heifer three years old and a she-goat three years old and a ram three years old and a turtle dove and a young pigeon."

He brought Him all these and split them down the middle and put each piece facing its neighbor but he did not split the birds. The birds of prey descended on the carcasses and Abram scared them away. Then it happened, the sun being ready to set, deep sleep fell on Abram and—look—a terror, a great dark falling on him.

He said to Abram "Surely you shall know that your seed shall be strangers in a land not theirs and they shall serve them, and they shall oppress them four hundred years. But also the nation which they shall serve, I am going to judge and afterward they shall leave with great wealth. You shall go to your fathers in peace. You shall be buried at a happy old age. And in the fourth generation they shall come back here since the Amorites' evil is not yet finished."

Then it happened, the sun having set and thick darkness fallen—look—a smoking oven and a fiery torch passed between these pieces. On that day Yahweh cut a covenant with Abram saying "To your seed I have given this land from the river of Egypt as far as the great river, the river Euphrates—the Kenite, the Kenizzite, the Kadmonite, the Hittite, the Perizzite, the Rephaim, the Amorite, the Canaanite, the Girgashite, and the Jebusite."

LUKE 1

The angel Gabriel was sent from God to a Galilean city named Nazareth to a virgin promised to a man named Joseph of the house of David. The virgin's name was Mary. Coming in on her he said "Rejoice, beloved! The Lord is with you."

She was much confused by the speech and wondered what kind of greeting this was.

The angel said to her "Do not be afraid, Mary. You are loved by God and—look—you shall conceive in your womb and bear a son and call his name Jesus. He shall be great, called Son of the Highest, and the Lord God shall give him the throne of David his father. He shall rule the house of Jacob to the ages and of his kingdom there shall be no end."

But Mary said to the angel "How will this happen? I know no man."

Answering the angel said to her "The Holy Spirit shall come over you and the strength of the Highest shall darken you so the holy thing being born shall be called Son of God. And—look—Elizabeth your cousin also conceived a son in her old age. This is the sixth month with her called barren since every word is possible with God."

Mary said "Look, the slave of the Lord. Let it be to me as your word was."

The angel left her.

GENESIS 18

Yahweh appeared to Abraham by the terebinths of Mamre while he was sitting at the door of the tent in the heat of day. He raised his eyes, looked and—look—three men standing by him. When he looked he ran from the door of the tent to meet them and said "Sir, if I've pleased you don't leave your slave please. Let a little water be drawn now. Wash your feet and lie under the tree. Let me feed your heart with a bit of bread. Then you can leave, having come to your slave."

They said "Do what you've said."

So Abraham ran into the tent to Sarah and said "Hurry, bring three seahs of meal, fine meal. Knead and make cakes." Then Abraham ran to the herd, took a good tender calf and gave it to a boy and he rushed to dress it. He took curds, milk and the dressed calf and set them before them. He stood by under the tree and they ate.

They said to him "Where's Sarah your wife?"

Abraham said "Look, in the tent."

And He said "Surely I'll return to you at birth time and—look—a son to Sarah your wife."

Sarah was listening at the door of the tent, it being behind Him, and Abraham and Sarah being old—far gone in days—the ways of women had stopped in her and Sarah laughed to herself saying "Used up as I am shall pleasure come to me and my lord being old?"

Yahweh said to Abraham "Why did Sarah laugh

then saying 'Shall I really bear when I am old?' Is anything shut to Yahweh? At the right time I will return to you—the birth time—and Sarah a son."

Sarah denied, saying "I didn't laugh" as she was afraid.

He said "You did laugh" and the men stood up from there and looked toward Sodom.

Look, the same day two of them were going to a town about seven miles from Jerusalem named Emmaus and they were talking about all these things that had been and it happened—as they talked and reasoned Jesus himself caught up and went with them but their eyes were fixed not to know him.

He said "What words are you trading on a walk?"

They stood sad-faced. Then answering the one called Cleopas said "Are you the only one living in Jerusalem not to know what's happened there lately?"

He said "What things?"

They said "About Jesus the Nazarene who was a man—a prophet—strong in act and word before God and all the people and how the chief priests and our rulers handed him over to judgment of death and crucified him when we were hoping he was set to save Israel. But then with all that, this is the third day since all this happened and now some of our women have astonished us. They were at the tomb early and, not finding his body, they came saying they'd also seen a vision of angels who say he's living. And some of us went to the tomb and found it the way the women said but him they didn't see."

He said to them "O fools, slow of heart to believe all the prophets said. Wasn't it needed that Messiah suffer these things and enter into his glory?" And starting with Moses and all the prophets he interpreted to them the things concerning himself in all the scriptures.

They neared the town they were going to and he seemed to be going on so they begged him saying "Stay with us since it's almost evening—day's done."

He went in to stay with them and it happened—as he reclined with them having taken the bread he blessed it and having broken handed it to them.

Their eyes were opened and they knew him.

Then he disappeared from them.

They said to each other "Didn't our heart burn in us as he spoke to us on the road and opened the scriptures to us?" And getting up the same hour they returned to Jerusalem and found the eleven and those with them gathered together saying "The Lord was really raised and appeared to Simon!" Then they told the events of their walk and how he was known by them in the breaking of bread.

As they were telling these things he himself stood in their midst and said "Peace to you."

But terrified and afraid they thought they saw a ghost.

He said to them "Why are you troubled and why do you reason in your heart? See my hands and my feet—I am myself. Feel me and see. A ghost does not have flesh and bones which you see me having." But while they were still doubting for joy and wondering he said "Do you have any food here?"

They gave him part of a broiled fish and taking it before them he ate.

God tested Abraham. He said to him "Abraham!"
He said "Here."

He said "Take your son, the son you love, Isaac,
and go to Moriah. There burn him to Me on the hill I
will show you."

The next dawn Abraham saddled his ass, took his
two young men and Isaac his son and, chopping wood
for the burning, rose and set off toward the place God
had mentioned.

On the third day Abraham raised his eyes and saw
the place still far ahead. He said to his young men
"Wait here with the ass. I and the boy will go there
and worship and come back to you."

Abraham took the wood for the burning and put it
on Isaac his son. The fire and the cleaver he carried
himself in his own hand. Then the two of them went
on together.

Isaac spoke to Abraham his father. He said
"Father."

He said "Here, Son."

He said "Look, fire and wood but no sheep to
burn."

Abraham said "Son, God will provide a sheep to
burn."

The two of them went on together and came to
the place God had mentioned to him.

Abraham built an altar there. He stacked the

wood. He bound Isaac his son. He laid him on the altar
on the wood. Abraham reached out his hand and took
the cleaver to kill his son.

But Yahweh's angel spoke from heaven and said
"Abraham! Abraham!"

He said "Here."

The angel said "Don't reach your hand to the boy.
Do nothing to him. Now I know you fear God since
you did not grudge Me your son, the son you love."

Abraham raised his eyes and saw—look—a ram
caught in briars by his horns. Abraham went, took the
ram and burned it instead of his son. Then Abraham
named the place Yahweh-yireh, hence the saying today
"Yahweh seen on the mountain."

Having sung a hymn they went out to the Mount of Olives.

Then Jesus said to them "All of you shall stumble because of me tonight for it was written

'*I will strike down the shepherd*

And the sheep of the flock shall be scattered'

but after I am raised I will go before you to Galilee."

Answering Peter said to him "Even if all stumble because of you tonight I'll never stumble."

Jesus said to him "Amen I tell you that tonight before a cock crows three times you shall deny me."

Peter said to him "Even if I have to die with you I'll never deny you."

Also all the disciples said the same.

Then Jesus came with them to a tract called Gethsemane and said to the disciples "Sit down here till I go there and pray."

Taking Peter and the two sons of Zebedee he began to grieve and be harrowed. Then he said to them "My soul is anguished to death. Stay here and watch with me."

Going on a little he fell on his face praying and saying "My Father, if it can be let this cup pass from me. Still not as I will but as You."

He came to the disciples and found them sleeping and said to Peter "So you could not watch with me one hour? Watch and pray not to fall into trial for the spirit is ready but the flesh is sick."

Going away a second time he prayed saying "My Father, if this cannot pass unless I drink it let Your will be done."

Again he came and found them sleeping for their eyes were heavy.

Leaving them and going away again he prayed a third time saying the same word again.

Then he came to the disciples and said to them "Still asleep and resting? Look, the hour is coming and the Son of Man is betrayed to sinners' hands. Rise. Let's go. Look, my traitor is coming."

While he was still speaking—look—Judas, one of the twelve, came and with him a big crowd with swords and sticks from the chief priests and elders of the people. The traitor gave them a sign saying "Whomever I kiss it's him. Seize him."

At once approaching Jesus he said "Rejoice, Rabbi!" and kissed him hard.

But Jesus said to him "Friend, do what you came for."

Then approaching they laid their hands on Jesus and seized him.

GENESIS 34

Dinah, Leah's daughter whom she bore to Jacob, left to see some of the women of the land.

Shechem—the son of Hamor the Hivite, chief of the land—saw her, took her, lay with her and shamed her. His soul clung to Dinah the daughter of Jacob. He loved the girl and spoke to the girl's heart. So Shechem spoke to Hamor his father saying "Get me this girl for a wife."

Now Jacob had heard that he had soiled his daughter Dinah but his sons were with his cattle in the field so Jacob kept silent till they came.

Hamor, Shechem's father, went to Jacob to speak with him.

Jacob's sons came in from the field when they heard. The men were wild and furious because outrage had been done in Israel—lying with Jacob's daughter, not to be done.

Hamor spoke with them saying "The soul of my son Shechem is bound to your daughter. Please give her to him for a wife. Intermarry with us. Give us your daughters and take our daughters for yourselves. Live with us. The land being before you—live and move about in it, get holdings."

Shechem said to her father and brothers "Let me win favor in your eyes. What you say to me I'll give. Raise the bridal dowry high and I'll pay as you tell me but give me the girl for a wife."

Jacob's sons answered Shechem and Hamor his father deceitfully because he had soiled Dinah their sister. They said to them "We can't do this—give our sister to an uncircumcised man. It would be a disgrace to us. Only for this will we agree to you—if you will be circumcised like us, every male of you. Then we will give our daughters to you and we will take your daughters for ourselves. We will live with you and become one people. If you don't listen to us and be circumcised we'll take our daughter and go."

Their words seemed good in the eyes of Hamor and Shechem, Hamor's son. The boy did not delay to do the thing since he delighted in Jacob's daughter (he was honored more than all his father's house). So Hamor and Shechem his son came to the gate of their city and spoke to the men of their city saying "These men are peaceable with us. Let them live in the land and move about in it for—look—the land is wide enough on both hands for them. Let's take their daughters as wives for ourselves and give our daughters to them. Only for this will they agree to live with us and become one people—if every male of us is circumcised as they are circumcised. Won't all their cattle and property and every work-animal be ours? Just agree to them and they will live with us."

Every man that went out of the gate of his city listened to Hamor and Shechem his son and they were circumcised—every male that went out of the gate of his city.

It happened on the third day—they being sick—that Jacob's two sons Simeon and Levi (Dinah's brothers) each took his sword and came on the city safely and killed every male. They killed Hamor and

Shechem his son with the mouth of the sword. They took Dinah from Shechem's house and left.

Jacob's other sons came on the killed and sacked the city because they had soiled their sister. Their flocks, herds, asses, what was in the city and the field they took—and all their wealth and all their little ones and their wives they took captive and sacked everything in the house.

Jacob said to Simeon and Levi "You have troubled me making me stink among the natives of the land, among the Canaanite and Perizzite, and I—having few men—they will gather against me and strike me and I shall be destroyed, I and my house."

They said "Should he treat our sister like a whore?"

God said to Jacob "Rise. Go up to Bethel and live there. Make an altar to God who appeared to you as you fled from your brother Esau."

Jacob said to his household and all who were with him "Cast off the strange gods from among you and clean yourselves and change your clothes. Let's rise and go up to Bethel. There I'll make an altar to God who answered me in my day of misery and was with me in the way I went."

They gave Jacob all the strange gods in their hand and the rings in their ears.

Jacob hid them under the terebinth near Shechem and they went.

The terror of God was on the cities round them. They did not chase after Jacob's sons.

GENESIS 32

In the night Jacob rose, took his two wives, his two slave girls and his eleven sons and crossed the ford of Jabbok. When he had carried them all across he sent his belongings.

Then Jacob was alone and some man wrestled with him there till daybreak.

When He saw that He could not win against him He struck him in the pit of his thigh so that Jacob's hip unsocketed as He wrestled with him. Then He said "Let me go. It is daybreak."

He said "I will not let go till you bless me."

He said to him "What is your name?"

He said "Jacob."

He said "Your name shall be Jacob no more but Israel. You have fought gods and men and won."

Jacob said "Tell me your name please."

He said "Why ask My name?" and blessed him there.

So Jacob called the place Peniel, *face of God*, "for I saw God face to face and my soul endured" and the sun struck him as he passed Penuel limping on his hip.

Another time Jesus showed himself to the disciples by the sea of Tiberias—showed himself this way.

Simon Peter was there with Thomas called "Twin," Nathanael from Cana in Galilee, the sons of Zebedee and two more of his disciples. Simon Peter said "I'm going out fishing."

The others said "We're coming with you." So they went out and got in the boat. But all night they caught nothing.

Then when day broke Jesus stood on the shore though none of them knew it was Jesus.

He called to them "Boys, anything to eat?"

They said "No."

So he said to them "Cast the net to starboard—you'll find them."

They cast and the crowd of fish was so big they couldn't haul it.

Then the disciple whom Jesus loved said to Peter "It's the Lord."

When Simon Peter heard it was the Lord he cinched up his shirt—under it he was naked—and threw himself into the sea.

The others came on in the little boat towing the net of fish—they were only a hundred yards or so from land—and when they landed they saw a charcoal fire laid with fish on it and bread.

Jesus said to them "Bring some of the fish you caught."

So Peter got up and hauled in the net full of big fish—a hundred and fifty-three and with all the number still the net was not torn.

Jesus said "Come eat breakfast."

Not one of the disciples dared ask "Who are you?" knowing it was the Lord.

Jesus came over, took the bread and gave it to them. Also the fish.

This was the third time Jesus showed himself to the disciples after being raised from the dead.

While Moses was herding flock for Jethro his father-in-law, the priest of Midian, he led the flock to the far side of the desert and came to God's mountain, to Horeb, and Yahweh's angel appeared to him in a blaze of fire from the heart of a thorn.

He looked and—look—the thorn was burning with fire and the thorn was not burnt and Moses said "I will turn now and see this great sight, why the thorn is not burned."

Yahweh saw that he turned to see and God called to him from the heart of the thorn and said "Moses, Moses."

He said "Here."

He said "Stay back. Take your shoes off your feet for the place you stand on is holy ground." And He said "I am the God of your father, the God of Abraham, the God of Isaac and the God of Jacob."

Moses hid his face. He feared seeing God.

Yahweh said "Surely I have seen the pain of my people in Egypt and have heard their cry because of their foremen for I know their sorrows and have come down to free them from the hand of the Egyptians and bring them up from that land to a good wide land, to a land streaming milk and honey—to the land of the Canaanite, the Hittite, the Amorite, the Perizzite, the Hivite and the Jebusite. And now—look—the cry of the children of Israel has come to Me and also I have seen the burden with which the Egyptians burden them. Now come and I will send you to Pharaoh and you bring My people the children of Israel out of Egypt."

Moses said to God "Who am I to go to Pharaoh and bring the children of Israel out of Egypt?"

He said "I will be with you and this is the sign I have sent you—in bringing the people out of Egypt you shall serve God on this mountain."

Moses said to God "Look, I come to the children of Israel and say to them 'The God of your fathers has sent me to you' and they will say to me 'What is His name?' What shall I say to them?"

God said to Moses "I Am What I Am." He said "So you shall say to the children of Israel 'I Am has sent me to you.'" And God again said to Moses "So you shall say to the children of Israel 'Yahweh the God of your fathers, the God of Abraham, the God of Isaac and the God of Jacob has sent me to you'—this My name forever and this My title for generation and generation. Go call the elders of Israel and say to them 'Yahweh the God of your fathers has appeared to me, the God of Abraham, Isaac and Jacob saying "Surely I have visited you and—what is done to you in Egypt!—I will bring you up from the pain of Egypt to the land of the Canaanite, the Hittite, the Amorite, the Perizzite, the Hivite and the Jebusite, to a land streaming milk and honey."' They shall listen to your voice and you shall come in—you and the elders of Israel—to the king of Egypt and you shall say to him 'Yahweh the God of the Hebrews has met us and now let us go please three days' journey into the desert and let us sacrifice to Yahweh our God.' I know that the king of Egypt will not let you go, not even by a strong hand, so I will extend My hand and strike Egypt with all My wonders which I will do in its presence and afterward he shall send you away. I will favor this people in the eyes of Egypt and it shall happen—when you go you shall not go empty but each woman shall ask from her neighbor and from the guest in her house pieces of silver and pieces of gold and clothes and you shall put them on your sons and daughters and plunder Egypt."

Moses answered and said "Look, they will not believe me and will not listen to my voice. They will say 'Yahweh has not appeared to you.'"

Yahweh said to him "What is this in your hand?"

He said "A stick."

He said "Throw it to the ground."

He threw it to the ground and it became a snake and Moses ran ahead of it.

Yahweh said to Moses "Reach out your hand and take it by the tail."

He reached out his hand and caught it and it became a stick in his hand.

"So they may believe Yahweh the God of their fathers has appeared to you—the God of Abraham, the God of Isaac and the God of Jacob." And again Yahweh said to him "Now put your hand in your breast."

He put his hand in his breast, took it out and—look—his hand was leprous like snow.

He said "Put back your hand in your breast."

He put back his hand in his breast, took it out and—look—it had turned like his flesh again.

"It shall happen—if they will not believe you and will not listen to the voice of the first sign they shall believe the voice of the later sign. And it shall happen—if they will not believe even these two signs and listen to your voice you shall take river water and pour on dry land and the water which you take from the river shall become blood on the dry land."

Moses said to Yahweh "O Lord, I am not a man of words neither yesterday nor now since Your speaking. I am heavy-mouthed and heavy-tongued."

Yahweh said to him "Who made the mouth on man? Or who makes dumb or deaf or seeing or blind?—not I Yahweh? Now go and I will be with your mouth and teach you what you shall say."

He said "Oh Lord, send the hand You will send."

Yahweh's anger burned against Moses and He said "Do I not know Aaron your brother the Levite?—that he can surely speak? And also—look—he is coming out to meet you and shall see you and be glad at heart and you shall speak to him and put words in his mouth and I will be with your mouth and his mouth and teach you what you shall do. He shall speak to the people for you and—it shall happen—he shall be a mouth for you and you shall be a god for him. This stick you shall take in your hand with which you shall do the signs."

Moses went back to Jethro his father-in-law and said to him "Let me go please back to my people in Egypt and see if they are alive."

Jethro said to Moses "Go in peace."

And Yahweh said to Moses in Midian "Go back to Egypt for all the men are dead—those wanting your life."

Moses took his wife and his sons and mounted them on an ass and returned to the land of Egypt and Moses took God's stick in his hand.

Yahweh said to Moses "When you return to Egypt see all the wonders I have put in your hand and do them for Pharaoh. But I will harden his heart and he shall not send the people away and you shall speak to Pharaoh 'Yahweh says "My son, My firstborn, is Israel and I say to you 'Send My son away and let him serve Me.' You refused to send him. Look, I am going to kill your son, your firstborn." ' "

It happened on the way in the camp—Yahweh met him and tried to kill him.

Zipporah took a flint and cut off her son's fore-skin and touched it to his feet and said "You are a bride-groom of blood to me."

And He let Moses go.

Then she said "A bridegroom of blood by circum-cision."

JOHN 8

The Jews said to him "Aren't we right to say you're Samaritan and have a demon?"

Jesus said "I have no demon but I honor my Father. You dishonor me. I am not seeking glory for me. There is One who seeks though and is judging. Amen amen if a man keeps my word he shall never in any way see death."

The Jews said to him "Now we know you have a demon. Abraham died and the prophets and you say 'If a man keeps my word he shall never in any way taste death.' Are you greater than Abraham our father who died? Or the prophets who died? Who are you?"

Jesus said "If I glorify myself my glory would be nothing. My Father glorifies me. You say 'He is our God.' You do not know Him. I know Him. If I said I did not know Him I'd be lying like you. I know Him and I keep His word. Abraham your father was glad to see my day. He saw it and laughed."

So the Jews said to him "You're not even fifty and you've seen Abraham?"

Jesus said to them "Amen amen I tell you before Abraham was I am."

They took up rocks to throw at him but he hid himself and left the Temple.

Moses said to Yahweh "Look, You say to me 'Bring this people up' but You have not told me whom You will send with me yet You have said 'I know you by name and you have also won favor in My eyes.' Now please if I have won favor in Your eyes show me please Your ways so I may know You and win favor in Your eyes. Consider that this people is Your nation."

He said "My face shall go with you and I will give you rest."

He said to Him "If Your face is not prepared to go don't bring us up from here. How can it be known now that I have won favor in Your eyes?—I and Your people. Isn't it in Your going with us that we are separate—I and Your people—from all nations on the face of the earth?"

Yahweh said to Moses "I will also do this thing you have said for you have won favor in My eyes and I know you by name."

He said "Show me please Your glory."

He said "I will make all My majesty pass before your face and I will proclaim the name of Yahweh in your face and will favor whom I favor and cherish whom I cherish." And He said "You cannot see My face—no man can see Me and live." Yahweh said "Look, a place near Me. You shall stand on a rock and it shall happen when My glory passes—I will put you in a hole in the rock and lay My hand over you as I pass. Then I will lift My hand and you shall see My back but

My face cannot be seen." Yahweh said to Moses "Cut yourself two tablets of stone like the first and I will write on the tablets the words that were on the first tablets which you broke. Be ready in the morning and come up in the morning to Mount Sinai and put yourself near Me there on the top of the mountain. No man shall come with you and no man shall be seen on all the mountain. Flocks and herds shall not feed near the mountain."

He cut two tablets of stone like the first and Moses rose early in the morning and went up Mount Sinai as Yahweh had ordered him. In his hands he took two tablets of stone.

Yahweh descended in the cloud and stood there with him and proclaimed the name of Yahweh. Yahweh passed before his face and proclaimed "Yahweh, Yahweh—a loving God, kind, slow to anger, full of mercy and truth, keeping mercy for thousands, forgiving wrong and trespass and sin but not entirely leaving guilt unpunished, visiting the wrong of fathers on children, on children of children to the third and fourth generation."

Moses quickly bowed to the earth and prostrated himself. He said "Now if I have won favor in Your eyes, O Lord, let the Lord please go in our midst—it is a stiff-necked people. Forgive our wrong and our sin and take us as a possession."

He said "Look, I am cutting a covenant before all your people. I will do wonderful things which have not been done in all the earth and among all nations. All the people among whom you go shall see the work of Yahweh for it is terrible what I am about to do with you."

On the first day of the week Mary the Magdalene came early while it was still dark to the tomb and saw that the stone had been taken from the tomb. So she ran to Simon Peter and the other disciple whom Jesus loved and said to them "They took the Lord from the tomb and we don't know where they put him."

So Peter came out and the other disciple and went to the tomb. The two ran together but the other disciple ran on quicker than Peter, got there first and leaning saw the linen lying there. But he didn't go in.

So Simon Peter arrived following him and went into the tomb and saw the linen lying there and the kerchief that was on his head not lying with the linen but to one side bundled in one place.

So then the other disciple went in, the one who had got to the tomb first and saw and believed (for they didn't yet understand the scripture that he must rise from the dead).

So the disciples left again for their home.

But Mary stood by the tomb outside crying. And as she cried she leaned into the tomb and saw two angels in white sitting one at the head and one at the feet of where Jesus' body had lain.

They said to her "Woman, why cry?"

She said to them "They took my Lord and I don't know where they put him."

Saying that she turned round and saw Jesus standing, not that she knew it was Jesus.

Jesus said to her "Woman, why cry? Whom do you want?"

She thinking it was the gardener said to him "Sir, if you carried him off tell me where you put him and I'll take him."

Jesus said to her "Mary."

Turning she said to him in Hebrew "*Rabboni*" which means "Teacher."

Jesus said to her "Stop holding me for I haven't yet gone up to the Father. But go to my brothers and tell them 'I'm going up to my Father and your Father, my God and your God.' "

Mary the Magdalene came to the disciples announcing "I've seen the Lord" and that he had said these things to her.

Then the spirit of Yahweh came over Jephthah and he went through Gilead and Manasseh and on through Mizpah of Gilead and from Mizpah of Gilead he went to the children of Ammon. And Jephthah vowed a vow to Yahweh and said "If You will surely give the children of Ammon to my hand then whatever comes out the doors of my house to meet me when I come back in triumph from the children of Ammon shall be Yahweh's and I will offer it as burnt offering." Then Jephthah went over to the children of Ammon to fight them and Yahweh gave them to his hand and he struck them with huge slaughter from Aroer to where you come to Minnith—twenty cities—as far as Abel-keramim.

So the children of Ammon were defeated before the children of Israel.

Then Jephthah came to Mizpah to his house and—look—his daughter came out to meet him with tambours and dances and she his only child. He had no son or daughter but her.

It happened when he saw her—he tore his clothes and said "Alas, my daughter. You have brought me down and you are one of them that hurt me. For I have opened my mouth to Yahweh and cannot go back."

She said to him "My father, you have opened your mouth to Yahweh. Do to me what has gone out of your mouth since Yahweh has avenged you on your enemies the children of Ammon." And she said to her father "Let this thing be done for me—let me alone two months to go and wander on the mountains and wail my virginity, I and my women."

He said "Go" and sent her away two months.

She went with her women and wailed her virginity on the mountains.

It happened at the end of two months—she returned to her father who did to her the vow he had vowed.

She knew no man.

Miriam and Aaron spoke against Moses because of the Cushite he married (he had married a Cushite). They said "Has Yahweh really spoken only through Moses? Hasn't He also spoken through us?"

Yahweh heard.

But the man Moses was very patient, more than all men on the face of the earth.

Suddenly Yahweh spoke to Moses, Aaron and Miriam—"Come out, you three, to the tent of meeting."

The three went out.

Then Yahweh came down in a pillar of cloud and stood at the door of the tent. He called Aaron and Miriam and they both came forward. He said "Please hear My words. If there is a prophet among you, I Yahweh will make Myself known to him in a vision, in a dream I will speak with him. My slave Moses is not such a one. In all My house he is faithful. Mouth to mouth I talk with him plainly and not in dark sayings. He sees the shape of Yahweh. Then were you not afraid to speak against My slave, against Moses?" Yahweh's anger flamed and He left. The cloud lifted off the tent.

And look, Miriam leprous as snow.

Aaron turned to Miriam and—look—she was leprous. Aaron said to Moses "Oh my lord, please don't lay sin on us though we've made fools of ourselves and sinned. Please don't leave her like a dead child born to its mother, half its flesh gone."

Moses pled with Yahweh saying "Oh God, I beg You heal her. I beg."

Yahweh said to Moses "If her own father had merely spat in her face wouldn't she bear shame for seven days? Let her shut herself up seven days outside the camp. Then let her be brought in."

So Miriam was shut up outside camp for seven days and the people did not move till Miriam was brought back. Then the people set out from Hazeroth and camped in the desert of Paran.

JOHN 9

Passing by Jesus saw a man blind since birth.

His disciples asked him "Rabbi, who sinned?—this man or his parents—that he was born blind?"

Jesus answered "Neither this man nor his parents sinned but that God's works be shown in him. While it is day we must do the work of Him that sent me—night is coming when no one can work. When I'm in the world I'm the light of the world." Saying that he spat on the ground and made clay with the spit and put the clay on his eyes and said to him "Go wash in the pool of Siloam" (which means *Sent*).

So he went, washed and came back seeing.

The neighbors and those who had seen him before—that he was a beggar—said "Isn't this the man who sat and begged?" Some said "This is he." Others said "No but it's like him."

He said "I am."

So they said to him "How were your eyes opened?"

He answered by saying "The man named Jesus made clay and anointed my eyes and told me 'Go to Siloam and wash' so going and washing I saw."

They said to him "Where is he?"

He said "I don't know."

They led him to the Pharisees—the once-blind man. Now it was a sabbath day when Jesus made the clay and opened his eyes so the Pharisees asked him again how he saw.

He said to them "He put clay on my eyes, I washed and I see."

So some of the Pharisees said "This man is not from God since he doesn't keep the sabbath." But others said "How can a sinful man do such signs?" and there was a split between them. So they said to the blind man again "What do you say about him since he opened your eyes?"

He said "He's a prophet."

But the Jews did not believe him—that he was blind and saw—till they called the parents of the one who had seen and asked them saying "Is this your son whom you say was born blind? How does he now see?"

His parents answered "We know that this is our son and that he was born blind but how he sees now we don't know or who opened his eyes we don't know. Ask him. He's of age. He'll speak for himself." His parents said these things since they feared the Jews for the Jews had already agreed that if anyone called him Messiah he would be put out of the synagogue. Thus the parents said "He's of age. Ask him."

So a second time they called the man who was blind and said to him "Give God the glory. We know that this man is sinful."

He answered "Whether he's sinful I don't know. I know one thing—that I was blind, now I see."

So they said to him "What did he do to you? How did he open your eyes?"

He answered them "I told you already and you didn't listen. Why do you want to hear again? You too want to become his disciples?"

They abused him by saying "You're a disciple of that man but we're disciples of Moses. We know that God has spoken through Moses but this man—we don't know where he comes from."

The man answered by saying to them "The wonderful thing here is that you don't know where he comes from but he opened my eyes. We know that God doesn't hear sinners but if anyone is godfearing and does His will He hears that man. From the beginning it was unheard of that anyone opened the eyes of a man born blind. If this man wasn't from God he couldn't do anything."

They answered by saying to him "You were born steeped in sin and you teach us?" and they threw him out.

Jesus heard that they threw him out and finding him said "Do you believe in the Son of Man?"

He answered by saying "Who is he, sir, so I may believe in him?"

Jesus said to him "You have both seen him and the one talking with you is he."

He said "I believe, sir" and knelt to him.

Joshua called the twelve men he had prepared from the sons of Israel—one man from each tribe—and Joshua said to them "Cross ahead of the ark of Yahweh your God to the middle of the Jordan and each man lift one stone on his shoulder according to the number of tribes of Israel's sons so this may be a sign among you for your children will ask tomorrow 'What do you mean by these stones?' Then you shall say to them 'Because the waters of the Jordan were cut off in the presence of the ark of Yahweh's covenant when it crossed the Jordan—the waters of the Jordan were cut off!—then these stones shall be a memory to Israel's sons forever.'"

The sons of Israel did what Joshua ordered. They lifted twelve stones from the middle of the Jordan as Yahweh told Joshua, according to the number of tribes of Israel's sons, and carried them over with them to the camp and put them down there.

Then Joshua set up twelve more stones in the middle of the Jordan where the priests' feet stood who carried the ark of the covenant.

They have stayed there to this day.

Thomas—one of the twelve called "Twin"—was not with them when Jesus came. So the other disciples said to him "We've seen the Lord."

But he said to them "Unless I see in his hands the place for the nails and put my finger in the place for the nails and put my hand in his side I'll never believe."

After eight days his disciples were inside again and Thomas was with them.

Jesus came—the doors had been shut—and stood in the middle and said "Peace to you." Then he said to Thomas "Bring your finger here and see my hands. Bring your hand and put it in my side. Don't be doubting but believing."

Thomas answered "My Lord, my God!"

Jesus said to him "Have you believed because you've seen me? Happy are those not seeing yet believing."

1 SAMUEL 3

The boy Samuel served Yahweh under Eli the priest. Word from Yahweh was scarce in those days. There was no general vision. But it happened at that time—when Eli was lying in his place (his eyes had started dimming so he couldn't see though God's lamp was not yet out) and Samuel was lying in Yahweh's temple where the ark of God was—that Yahweh called Samuel.

He said "Here." Then he ran to Eli and said "Here I am. You called me."

He said "I didn't call. Lie back down."

He went and lay down.

Yahweh called again "Samuel."

Samuel rose and went to Eli and said "Here I am. You called me."

He said "I didn't call, son. Lie back down."

Now Samuel did not yet know Yahweh nor had word from Yahweh been revealed to him.

But Yahweh called Samuel again a third time.

He rose and went to Eli and said "Here I am. You called me."

So Eli saw that Yahweh called the boy and Eli said to Samuel "Go lie down and let it be. If He calls you you say 'Speak, Yahweh. Your slave is listening.' "

Samuel went and lay in his place.

Yahweh came, stood and called as before "Samuel, Samuel."

Samuel said "Speak. Your slave is listening."

Yahweh said to Samuel "Look, I will do a thing in Israel so everyone who hears it both his ears shall burn. On that day I will do against Eli all I have said about his house from start to finish. I have told him I will punish his house forever for the evil he knew of—that his sons were cursing God and he did not stop them. Thus I have sworn to the house of Eli that the evil of Eli's house shall not be canceled by sacrifice or offering forever."

Samuel lay till morning. Then he opened the doors of Yahweh's house but Samuel was afraid to tell the vision to Eli.

So Eli called Samuel. He said "Samuel my son."

He said "Here."

He said "What is the word He spoke to you? Please don't hide it from me—God do so to you and more if you hide from me any word of all He spoke to you."

Samuel told him all the words and did not hide from him.

Then he said "It is Yahweh. Whatever is right in His eyes let Him do."

Samuel grew and Yahweh proved with him and did not let any of his words fall to earth.

So all Israel knew from Dan to Beersheba that Samuel was confirmed as a prophet of Yahweh.

Jesus came to Nazareth where he was reared and went as usual on the sabbaths to the synagogue and stood to read. A scroll of the prophet Isaiah was handed to him and unrolling the scroll he found the place where it was written

The spirit of the Lord is on me
Because He anointed me
To cheer the poor.
He has sent me announcing release to captives,
Sight to the blind,
Release to the bruised,
Announcing the welcome year of the Lord.

Rolling up the scroll and giving it to the keeper he sat and the eyes of all in the synagogue were fixed on him. He began to say to them "Today this scripture is fulfilled in your ears."

All witnessed to him and wondered at the graceful words coming out of his mouth. They said "Isn't this Joseph's son?"

He said to them "Surely you'll tell me this proverb 'Doctor, cure yourself: whatever we hear happening in Capernaum do here at home.'" Then he said "Amen I tell you no prophet is welcome at home. But I tell you honestly there were many widows in Israel in the days of Elijah when heaven was locked for three years and six months while a great famine came over the land and to not one of them was Elijah sent but to Sarepta in Sidon to a widow woman. And many lepers were in Israel under Elisha the prophet and not one of them was cleansed except Naaman the Syrian."

All in the synagogue were filled with rage hearing these things and getting up they threw him out of the town and led him to the brow of the hill on which their town had been built to pitch him down.

But he passing through their midst went on.

Now Samuel was dead and all Israel had mourned him and buried him in Ramah his own city. And Saul had put those that had demons and the wizards out of the country.

The Philistines gathered, came and camped at Shunem.

Saul gathered all Israel and they camped at Gilboa. When Saul saw the army of the Philistines he was afraid and his heart shook hard. Then Saul asked Yahweh but Yahweh did not answer either in dreams or by Urim or by prophets. So Saul said to his slaves "Find me a woman who has a demon so I may go to her and ask her."

His slaves said to him "Look, there is a woman who has a demon in Endor."

Saul disguised himself, put on other clothes and went—he and two men with him—and they came to the woman at night and said "Conjure for me by your demon and raise for me whomever I name to you."

The woman said to him "Look, you know what Saul has done—how he has cut from the land those with demons and the wizards—so why are you setting traps for my life to make me die?"

Saul swore to her by Yahweh saying "By the life of Yahweh no punishment will fall on you for this.

So the woman said "Whom shall I raise for you?"

He said "Bring up Samuel for me."

When the woman saw Samuel she cried out in a loud voice and the woman spoke to Saul saying "Why have you deceived me—you yourself being Saul?"

The king said to her "Don't be afraid. What do you see?"

The woman said to Saul "I see a god coming up from the earth."

He said to her "What is his shape?"

She said "An old man coming up covered in a robe."

Saul knew it was Samuel so he pressed his face to the ground and worshipped.

Samuel said to Saul "Why have you afflicted me bringing me up?"

Saul said "I am in bad trouble—the Philistines are fighting me and God has turned from me and answers me no more neither by prophets nor by dreams so I have called you to tell me what I must do."

Samuel said "Why should you ask me when Yahweh has turned from you and become your enemy? Yahweh has done to you what He spoke by my hand. Yahweh has torn the kingdom from your hand and given it to your neighbor. Since you did not listen to the voice of Yahweh or execute the fire of His wrath on Amalek so Yahweh has done this thing to you today that Yahweh may give Israel along with you into the hand of the Philistines. Tomorrow you and your sons shall be with me. Yahweh shall also give the army of Israel into the hand of the Philistines."

At once Saul fell prostrate his whole length on the ground and was terrified at Samuel's words. There was no strength in him for he had not eaten bread all day and all night.

The woman came to Saul and when she saw he was so frightened she said to him "Look, your servant heard your voice. I took my soul in my hand and listened to the words you said to me. Now please listen also to the voice of your servant and let me put a bit of bread before you and you eat so there's strength in you when you go on your way."

He refused and said "I will not eat."

But when his slaves and the woman also pressed him then he listened to their voice and rose from the ground and sat on the bed.

Now the woman had a calf fattening in the house. She ran and killed it. She took meal, kneaded and baked unleavened cakes from it and set them before Saul and his slaves and they ate.

Then they rose and left the same night.

David again summoned all the choice men in Israel, thirty thousand. Then David rose and went with all his people from Baale-judah to bring up from there the ark of God which is called by the name of Yahweh of Hosts who sits on the cherubim upon it.

They set the ark of God on a new cart and brought it out of Abinadab's house on the hill. Uzzah and Ahio, Abinadab's sons, were driving the new cart with the ark of God. Ahio went ahead of the ark.

David and all the house of Israel were rejoicing before Yahweh with all their might with songs, lyres, harps, tambourines, rattles and crymbals.

When they came to Nacon's threshing floor Uzzah put out his hand to God's ark and held it for the oxen stumbled.

Then Yahweh's anger burned against Uzzah and God struck him there for his error. He died there by the ark of God.

David was angry that Yahweh had crashed in on Uzzah and that place is called Perez-uzzah, *the crashing in on Uzzah*, to this day. David was afraid of Yahweh that day and said "How shall the ark of Yahweh come to me?" So David did not want to bring the ark of God in to himself in David's city but David took it off to the house of Obed-edom the Gittite.

The ark of Yahweh stayed in the house of Obed-edom the Gittite three months and Yahweh blessed Obed-edom and all his household.

So King David was told "Yahweh has blessed the house of Obed-edom and all that belongs to him because of the ark of God."

Then David went and brought the ark of God up from Obed-edom's house to the city of David joyfully. It was like this—when the ones that carried the ark of Yahweh had walked six paces he sacrificed an ox and a fatling and David danced boldly before Yahweh (David was wearing a linen apron). So David and all the house of Israel brought the ark of Yahweh up with shouting and the sound of trumpets.

Then it was like this—when the ark of Yahweh entered David's city Michal, Saul's daughter, looked out the window and saw King David springing and dancing before Yahweh and she despised him in her heart.

But they brought the ark of Yahweh in and set it in its place in the middle of the tent David had pitched for it and David offered burnt offerings before Yahweh and peace offerings. When David had finished offering the burnt offering and peace offerings he blessed the people in the name of Yahweh of Hosts. Then he distributed among all the people—among the whole crowd of Israel both men and women—to each a loaf of bread, a ration of meat and a cake of raisins.

All the people left each to his house and David went back to bless his house.

Then Michal, Saul's daughter, came out to meet David and said "How glorious the king of Israel was today, stripping himself before the eyes of his servants' slavegirls as a common fool might strip himself."

David said to Michal "—Before Yahweh who picked me instead of your father and all his house to command me prince over Yahweh's people, over Israel. So I will dance before Yahweh and be even viler than this. I will be common in my own eyes and with the slave-girls you spoke of. With them I'll be honored."

Michal, Saul's daughter, had no child till the day of her death.

One of the Pharisees asked Jesus to eat with him and coming in to the Pharisee's house he lay down at table.

Then look, a woman from the city, a sinner, knowing he lay at the Pharisee's house, brought an alabaster bottle of ointment and standing behind by his feet and crying she began to wet his feet with tears and wiped them with the hair of her head and lovingly kissed his feet and anointed them with ointment.

But seeing, the Pharisee who invited him said to himself "If this man were a prophet he'd have known who and what kind of woman is touching him—she's a sinner."

Answering Jesus said to him "Simon, I've something to tell you."

He said "Teacher, tell on."

"A certain money-lender had two debtors. One owed five hundred denarii, the other fifty. Since they had no means to repay he generously forgave them both. Which of them then will love him more?"

Answering Simon said "I suppose him whom he forgave the more."

He said to him "You've judged right." Then turning to the woman he said to Simon "See this woman? I came into your house—you gave me no water on my feet. But this woman wet my feet with tears and wiped them with her hair. You gave me no kiss but this woman from when I came in never stopped lovingly kissing my feet. You didn't anoint my head with oil but this woman anointed my feet with ointment because of which, I tell you, her many sins have been forgiven since she loved much. But he for whom little is forgiven loves little." Then he said to her "Your sins have been forgiven."

The ones lying with him started saying to themselves "Who is this who even forgives sins?"

But he said to the woman "Your faith has saved you. Leave in peace."

Ahab told Jezebel all Elijah had done and about how he had killed all the prophets by sword.

Then Jezebel sent a messenger to Elijah saying "Let the gods do that to me and more if by now tomorrow I have not made your life like one of their lives."

He was afraid, rose and left for his life. He came to Beersheba which belongs to Judah and left his boy there. But he himself went a day's march into the desert, came and sat under a broom-shrub, asked of his life that he might die and said "Enough, O Yahweh! Take my life. I'm no better than my fathers." Then he lay and slept under a broom-shrub.

Then look, an angel touched him and said to him "Rise and eat."

He looked and—look—there was by his head a cake baked on hot stones and a jug of water. He ate, drank and lay again.

The angel of Yahweh came again a second time, touched him and said "Rise and eat. The trip is too much for you."

So he rose, ate and drank and went on the strength of that eating forty days and forty nights as far as the mountain of God, Horeb. He came to a cave and stayed there.

And look, Yahweh's word came to him and said to him "What are you doing here, Elijah?"

He said "I have been very zealous for Yahweh

God of Hosts for Israel's sons have abandoned Your
covenant. They have thrown down Your altars and
killed Your prophets by sword and I—I alone—am left
and they hunt my life to take it."

He said "Go out and stand on the mountain before Yahweh." And look, Yahweh passing by! And a
great strong wind tearing the mountains and crushing
the rocks to pieces before Yahweh. But Yahweh was
not in the wind and after the wind an earthquake but
Yahweh was not in the earthquake and after the earthquake fire but Yahweh was not in the fire and after the
fire a gentle whispering voice.

When Elijah heard it he wrapped his face in his
coat and went out and stood at the mouth of the cave.

And look, a voice came to him and said "What are
you doing here, Elijah?"

He said "I have been very zealous for Yahweh
God of Hosts. For Israel's sons have abandoned Your
covenant. They have thrown down Your altars and
killed your prophets by sword and I—I alone—am left
and they hunt my life to take it."

Yahweh said "Go. Return by way of the desert of
Damascus and when you arrive you shall anoint Hazael
king over Syria and you shall anoint Jehu son of
Nimshi king over Israel and you shall anoint Elisha son
of Shaphat of Abel-meholah prophet in your place. He
who escapes Hazael's sword Jehu shall kill. He who
escapes Jehu's sword Elisha shall kill. Still I will leave
seven thousand in Israel—all knees that have not
bowed to Baal, all mouths which have not kissed him."

So he left there and found Elisha son of Shaphat
while he was plowing twelve yoke of oxen before him—

he being with the twelfth. Elijah passed him and threw his coat over him.

He left the oxen, ran after Elijah and said "I beg you let me kiss my father and mother so I can follow you."

He said to him "Go. Return. What have I done for you?"

He turned from following him and took the yoke of oxen and killed them and boiled their meat with the yokes for fuel. He gave it to the people and they ate. Then he rose and followed Elijah and served him.

Arresting Peter too—during the days of unleavened bread—Herod put him in prison, delivering him to four squads of soldiers to guard him, meaning after Passover to bring him before the people. So on the one hand Peter was held in prison but on the other prayer was fervently offered by the community to God for him. So when Herod was about to bring him out that night Peter was sleeping between two soldiers bound with two chains and sentries were at the door guarding the prison.

And look, the Lord's angel came on him suddenly and light blazed in the room. Knocking Peter's side he woke him by saying "Rise. Hurry."

The chains on his hands fell off.

Then the angel said to him "Dress yourself and put on your sandals."

He did that.

So he told him "Throw your coat round you and follow me."

Going out he followed and did not know that the thing happening with the angel was true—he thought he saw a vision.

But passing through the first ward and the second they came to the iron gate leading to the city which opened by itself for them. Going out they went the length of one street.

At once the angel left him.

Peter having come to himself said "Now I know that the Lord really sent out His angel and freed me from Herod's hand and all the hope of the Jewish people."

Understanding he came to the house of Mary the mother of John surnamed Mark where many were gathered praying.

When he knocked at the porch door a maid came to listen named Rhoda. Knowing Peter's voice for joy she didn't open the porch but running in she announced that Peter stood on the porch.

They said to her "You're crazy."

But she insisted it was so.

So they said "It's his angel."

Still Peter went on knocking.

And opening they saw him and were stunned.

Signaling them with his hand to be silent he told them how the Lord led him from prison and he said "Announce these things to James and the brothers." Then leaving he went to another place.

One day Elisha went over to Shunem where there was a great lady who made him eat some bread. So it happened that whenever he went that way he turned off there to eat bread.

She said to her husband "Look please. I know he is a holy man from God coming our way continually. Please let's make a little room up on the walls and put there a bed for him, a table, a chair and a lamp so whenever he comes to us he can stay up there."

It happened one day when he came there—he turned off into the high room and slept. Then he said to Gehazi his boy "Call this Shunammite."

He called her and she stood before him.

He said to him "Please say to her 'Look. You have tended us with all this careful service. What can be done for you? Could we speak for you to the king or the general of the army?' "

But she said "I live among my people."

He said "What can be done for her then?"

Gehazi said "In fact she has no son and her husband is old."

He said "Call her."

He called her and she stood in the door.

Then he said "This season next year about spring you shall be hugging a son."

She said "No, my lord! Man from God, don't deceive your servant." But the lady conceived and had a son at that season—about spring—as Elisha had told her.

When the child was grown it happened one day that he went out to his father to the reapers. Then he said to his father "My head! My head!"

So he said to his boy "Carry him to his mother."

When he had lifted him and carried him to his mother he sat on her knees till noon. Then he died.

She climbed up, laid him on the man of God's bed, shut the door on him and went out. Then she called her husband and said "Please send me one of the boys and one of the asses so I can run to the man of God and return."

He said "Why go to him today? It's neither new moon nor sabbath."

She said "Peace." Then she saddled the ass and said to the boy "Lead on. Go ahead. Don't slow for my sake unless I tell you." Thus she set off and came to the man of God at Mount Carmel.

It happened when the man of God saw her opposite—he said to Gehazi his boy "Look, the Shunammite. Please run to meet her and say to her 'Is all well with you, well with your husband, well with the child?' "

She said "Well."

But when she came to the man of God on the mountain she clutched at his feet.

Gehazi approached to push her away.

But the man of God said "Let her be. Her soul is bitter to her though Yahweh has hid it from me and not told me."

Then she said "Did I ask my lord for a son? Didn't I say 'Don't deceive me?' "

He said to Gehazi "Cinch up your loins, take a stick in hand and go. If you meet any man don't bless him. If any man blesses you don't reply. Then lay my stick on the boy's face."

But the boy's mother said "By Yahweh's life, by your own soul's life I will not leave you."

So he rose and followed her.

Gehazi had gone on ahead of him and laid the stick on the boy's face but there was no voice or sign of life. So he went back to meet him and told him "The boy has not waked."

When Elisha entered the house—look—the boy was dead stretched on his bed. He went in, shut the door on them both and prayed to Yahweh. Then he got up, lay on the child and put his own mouth on his mouth, his own eyes on his eyes, his own hands on his hands and pressed himself upon him.

The boy's skin grew warm.

Then he got down and walked once back and forth in the house. Then he got up and pressed himself upon him.

The boy sneezed as many as seven times and opened his eyes.

He called Gehazi and said "Call this Shunammite."

So he called her and when she had come in to him he said "Take your son."

She came in, fell at his feet, bowed to the ground, took her son and left.

Now a certain man was sick—Lazarus from Bethany the town of Mary and Martha her sister. It was Mary who anointed the Lord with ointment and wiped his feet with her hair whose brother Lazarus was sick. So the sisters sent to him saying "Lord, look. He whom you love is sick."

But hearing that Jesus said "This sickness is not to death but for God's glory that the Son of God may be glorified through it." Now Jesus loved Martha and her sister and Lazarus. So when he heard he was sick then in fact he stayed in the place where he was two days. Then after this he said to the disciples "Let's go into Judea again."

The disciples said to him "Rabbi, just now the Jews were trying to stone you and again you're going there?"

Jesus answered "Aren't there twelve hours in the day? If a man walks by day he never stumbles because he sees the light of this world. But if a man walks by night he stumbles because the light is not in him." He said these things and after this he told them "Lazarus our friend has fallen asleep but I go so I may wake him."

His disciples said "Lord, if he has fallen asleep he will get well." Jesus had spoken of his death but they thought he spoke of the rest of sleep.

So then Jesus said to them plainly "Lazarus died.

And I am glad for your sake—so that you may believe—that I was not there. But let's go to him."

So Thomas called "Twin" said to his fellow disciples "Let's go too so we can die with him."

Coming then Jesus found him four days in the
tomb.

Now Bethany was near Jerusalem about two miles
off and many of the Jews had come to Martha and
Mary to console them about their brother.

So when Martha heard that Jesus was coming she
met him.

But Mary was sitting in the house.

Then Martha said to Jesus "Lord, if you had been
here my brother wouldn't have died but even now I
know that whatever you ask of God, God will give
you."

Jesus said to her "Your brother shall rise again."

Martha said to him "I know he will rise again in
the resurrection on the last day."

Jesus said to her "I am the resurrection and the
life. He that believes in me though he dies shall live
and everyone who lives and believes in me in no way
shall die forever. Do you believe this?"

She said to him "Yes, Lord. I have believed that
you are Messiah the Son of God coming into the
world." Having said this she went off and called Mary
her sister secretly saying "The master is here and calls
you."

When she heard she rose quickly and came to
him.

Now Jesus had not yet entered the town but was
in the place where Martha met him.

The Jews who were with her in the house consoling her, seeing Mary—how she rose quickly and went out—followed her, thinking "She is going to the tomb to weep there."

So when Mary came where Jesus was, seeing him she fell at his feet saying to him "Lord, if you had been here my brother would not have died."

When Jesus saw her weeping and the Jews who came with her weeping he howled in his soul and harrowed himself and said "Where have you laid him?"

They said to him "Lord, come and see."

Jesus wept.

So the Jews said "Look. He loved him." But some of them said "Couldn't he who opened the blind man's eyes have made this man not die?"

So Jesus howling in himself again came to the tomb. It was a cave and a stone was lying on it. Jesus said "Take back the stone."

Martha the sister of the one who had died said to him "Lord, he stinks. It's the fourth day."

Jesus said to her "Didn't I tell you that if you believed you shall see God's glory?"

So they took away the stone.

Jesus raised his eyes and said "Father, I thank You that You heard me. I knew that You always hear me but because of the crowd who stand round I said it so they may believe You sent me." And saying these things with a loud voice he cried "Lazarus, come out."

The one who had been dead came out bound feet and hands with shrouding and his face wrapped in a cloth.

Jesus said to them "Free him and let him go."

2 KINGS 9

When Jehu entered Jezreel and Jezebel heard she painted her eyes, decked her head and looked out the window. And as Jehu entered in by the gate she said "Is it peace, you Zimri who killed your master?"

He raised his face to the window and said "Who is with me? Who?"

Two or three eunuchs looked out at him.

He said "Throw her down."

So they threw her down and some of her blood spattered wall and horses and they trampled her.

Then when he had entered and eaten and drunk he said "Now see to this blighted woman and bury her. She is a king's daughter."

They went to bury her and found nothing there but skull and feet and the palms of her hands. So they came back and told him.

And he said "—The word of Yahweh which He spoke through the hand of His slave Elijah the Tishbite saying 'Round Jezreel dogs shall eat the meat of Jezebel. The carcass of Jezebel shall be like dung on the face of the field round Jezreel so they shall not say "This is Jezebel." ' "

Joseph, seventeen years old, was keeping the flock with his brothers—being a helper to the sons of Bilhah and Zilpah, his father's wives—and Joseph brought his father the talk about them, bad talk.

Israel loved Joseph more than all his sons because he was a son of his old age and he made him a fancy coat.

His brothers saw that their father loved him more than all his brothers. They hated him and could not speak peacefully to him.

Joseph dreamed a dream and told his brothers.

They still hated him.

He said to them "Now listen to this dream I've dreamed. Look, we were tying sheaves in the middle of the field and—look—my sheaf rose and then stood and—look—your sheaves moved round and bowed to my sheaf."

His brothers said to him "Will you really reign over us? Will you really rule us?" They went on hating him because of his dreams and his words.

He dreamed again another dream and told it to his brothers. "Look, I've dreamed a dream again. Look, the sun and moon and eleven stars were bowing to me." He told his father and his brothers.

His father scolded him and said "What is this dream you've dreamed? Shall we really come—I, your mother and brothers—and bow ourselves down flat to you?" His brothers were jealous of him but his father pondered the words.

Then his brothers went to herd their father's flock in Shechem.

Israel said to Joseph "Aren't your brothers herding in Shechem? Come I'll send you to them."

He said "Here I am."

So he said to him "Go now. See about the health of your brothers, the health of the flock and bring me back word" and he sent him from the Hebron valley.

He came to Shechem.

And a man found him—look, he was wandering in the fields—and asked him "What are you hunting?"

He said "I'm hunting my brothers. Please tell me where they're herding."

The man said "They've left here. I heard them say 'Let's go toward Dothan.'"

Joseph went after his brothers and found them in Dothan.

They saw him far off and before he came near them they plotted to kill him. They said each to his brother "Look, the master-dreamer's coming. Now come let's kill him and throw him into one of the pits. We'll say 'A wild beast has eaten him.' Then see what will become of his dreams!"

Reuben heard and saved him from their hands. He said "Don't let's strike him dead." Reuben said to them "Shed no blood. Throw him into this pit in the desert but don't lay a hand on him"—so he might save him from their hand and return him to their father.

It happened when Joseph came to his brothers—they stripped off Joseph's coat, the fancy tunic, took him and threw him into the pit (the pit was empty, no water in it). Then they sat to eat bread, raised their eyes and saw—look—a caravan of Ishmaelites coming from Gilead (their camels bearing gum, balm, ladanum) going to carry it down to Egypt.

Judah said to his brothers "What good is it if we kill our brother and hide his blood? Come, let's sell him to the Ishmaelites. Don't let our hand be on him—he's our brother, our flesh."

His brothers heard him.

But Midianite traders passed, hauled and lifted Joseph up from the pit and sold Joseph to the Ishmaelites for twenty pieces of silver.

They took Joseph to Egypt.

Reuben went back to the pit and—look—Joseph was not in the pit. He tore his clothes, went back to his brothers and said "The child's not there and I—where shall I go?"

They took Joseph's coat, slaughtered a billy goat and dipped the coat in the blood. They sent the fancy coat back to their father and said "We've found this. See now whether or not it's your son's coat."

He saw it and said "My son's coat! A wild beast has eaten him. Joseph is surely torn to bits." Jacob tore his clothes, put sackcloth on his loins and mourned his son many days.

All his sons rose and all his daughters to comfort him.

But he refused to be comforted and said "I will go down to my son mourning to Sheol." Thus his father wept for him.

The Midianites sold him in Egypt to Potiphar a eunuch of Pharaoh, chief of the stewards.

Yahweh was with Joseph. He was a prosperous

man and was in the house of his master the Egyptian.

His master saw that Yahweh was with him and that Yahweh blessed everything in his hand so Joseph won favor in his eyes, served him and he made him overseer of his house and put everything he had in his hand. It happened from the time he appointed him over his house and all he had—Yahweh blessed the Egyptian's house because of Joseph and Yahweh's blessing was on all he had in house and field. He left all he had in Joseph's hand and noticed nothing but the bread he ate.

Now Joseph was beautiful in body and face so it happened after these things that his master's wife raised her eyes to Joseph and said "Lie with me."

He refused and said to his master's wife "Look, with me here my master doesn't even know what's in the house. He's given all he has into my hand. He is not greater in this house than I and has not withheld anything from me but you since you are his wife. How can I do this great wrong and sin against God?" And it happened that though she spoke to Joseph day by day he did not listen to her—to lie by her and be with her. Then it happened about this time—he came into the house to do his work and there was no house servant there in the house.

She seized him by his coat saying "Lie with me."

He left his coat in her hand and fled outside.

It happened when she saw he had left his coat in her hand and fled outside—she called the men of her house and said to them "Look, he's brought in a Hebrew to trifle with us. He came in to me to lie with me and I cried in a loud voice and it happened that when he heard me screaming he left his coat near me and fled outside." She kept his coat near her till his master came home. Then she said the same thing "The Hebrew slave you've brought in to trifle with me came into me and it happened when I screamed he left his coat near me and fled outside."

It happened when his master heard his wife's words "Your slave did as I'm saying to me"—his anger burned. Joseph's master took him and put him in prison, the place where the king's prisoners were imprisoned.

He was there in prison and Yahweh extended him kindness and gave him favor in the eyes of the prison warden. And the prison warden put in Joseph's hand all the prisoners in prison. All that was done there he did. Since Yahweh was with him the warden did not oversee anything and all he did Yahweh blessed.

It happened after these things—the cupbearer and the baker to the king of Egypt sinned against their lord the king of Egypt.

Pharaoh was angry with his two officers, the chief cupbearer and the chief baker, so he put them into custody in the chief steward's house in the prison where Joseph was held.

The chief steward put Joseph with them and he served them (they were in custody for days).

They dreamed a dream both of them each his own dream in the night, each dream with its meaning—the cupbearer and the baker to the king of Egypt who were held in prison.

Joseph came in to them in the morning and saw them—look—dejected. He asked Pharaoh's officers who were with him in prison in his master's house "Why are your faces troubled today?"

They said to him "We've dreamed a dream and there's no interpreter."

Joseph said to them "Don't interpretations come from God? Tell me now."

So the chief cupbearer told his dream to Joseph. "In my dream—look—a vine before me and on the vine three branches. When it budded its blossoms came out and its branches ripened to grapes. Pharaoh's cup was in my hand so I took the grapes, squeezed them into Pharaoh's cup and put the cup into Pharaoh's hand."

Joseph said to him "This is its interpretation. The three branches are three days. In three more days Pharaoh shall lift your head and return you to your place and you shall put Pharaoh's cup into his hand as before when you were cupbearer. But if you can, remember me when it's well with you. Treat me kindly please and mention me to Pharaoh. Get me out of this house for I was really stolen from the land of the Hebrews and even here I haven't done a thing that they should put me in the pit."

The chief baker saw that the interpretation was good and said to Joseph "I also was in my dream when—look—three baskets of white bread were on my head and in the top basket some of all Pharaoh's foods, baker's work. And birds were eating them from the basket on my head."

Joseph answered "This is its interpretation. The three baskets are three days. In three more days Pharaoh shall lift your head from your shoulders and impale you on a tree and the birds shall eat your flesh from you."

It happened on the third day, Pharaoh's birthday—he gave a feast for all his servants and lifted the head of the chief cupbearer and the chief baker in the midst of his servants. He returned the chief cupbearer to his place—he put the cup into Pharaoh's hand—but the chief baker he impaled as Joseph had interpreted to them.

Still the chief cupbearer did not remember Joseph. He forgot him.

It happened at the end of two full years. Pharaoh was dreaming and—look—he was standing by the Nile and—look—seven cows were coming out of the Nile handsome and fat and feeding in the reeds. And look, seven other cows coming out of the Nile after them ugly and gaunt. They stood by the cows on the bank of the Nile and the ugly gaunt cows were eating the handsome fat cows. Then Pharaoh woke. But he slept and dreamed a second time and—look—seven ears of grain growing on one stalk plump and good. But look, seven ears of grain thin and parched by the east wind were sprouting behind them and the thin ears were swallowing the seven plump full ears. Pharaoh woke and—look—it was a dream. It happened in the morning his spirit was troubled. He summoned all the magicians of Egypt and all its wise men. Then Pharaoh told them his dreams.

But none could interpret them to Pharaoh.

The chief cupbearer spoke to Pharaoh. "Today I recall my sins. Once Pharaoh was angry with his servants and put me in custody in the chief steward's house, me and the chief baker. We dreamed a dream one night, I and he—each dreamed a dream with its own interpretation. A Hebrew boy was with us, a slave of the chief steward, and we told him. He interpreted our dreams, interpreted each his own dream. And it happened as he interpreted to us so it was. He returned me to my place and impaled him."

Pharaoh summoned Joseph.

They made him run from the dungeon. He shaved himself, changed his clothes and came in to Pharaoh.

Pharaoh said to Joseph "I've dreamed a dream and no one can interpret it. I've heard about you—you can hear a dream and interpret it."

Joseph answered Pharaoh "Not I. God will answer Pharaoh generously."

Pharaoh said to Joseph "In my dream—look—I was standing on the bank of the Nile and—look—seven cows were coming out of the river fat and handsome and feeding in the reeds. And look, seven other cows were coming out after them gaunt and very ugly (I have not seen their like for badness in all the land of Egypt). The gaunt and ugly cows ate the first seven cows yet when they went into them it couldn't be seen that they'd gone into them—their appearance was as ugly as before. Then I woke. Then I looked back into my dream and—look—seven ears of grain growing on one stalk plump and good and—look—seven withered thin ears parched by the east wind were sprouting behind them and the thin ears were swallowing the good ears. I spoke to the magicians but none could explain it to me."

Joseph said to Pharaoh "Pharaoh's dream is one. God has revealed to Pharaoh what He is about to do. The seven good cows are seven years and the seven good ears are seven years—it is one dream. The seven gaunt ugly cows coming out after them are seven years and the seven thin ears parched by the east wind shall be seven years of famine. That's what I have to tell Pharaoh. God has showed Pharaoh what He is about to do. Look, seven years of great plenty are coming through all Egypt. Seven years of famine shall rise after them and the plenty in Egypt shall be forgot. Famine shall ravage the land and plenty shall be unknown from that famine onward for it shall be very hard. And as for Pharaoh's dream being repeated twice—that's because the thing is settled with God and God is rushing to do it. Let Pharaoh look for a keen wise man and put him over Egypt and let Pharaoh appoint overseers to the land and organize Egypt in the seven years of plenty. Let them save all the food of these coming good years and pile up grain under Pharaoh's hand for food in the cities. Let the food be a stock for the land for the seven years of famine in Egypt so the land not be cut down by famine."

The word was good in Pharaoh's eyes and the eyes of all his servants. Pharaoh said to his servants "Can we find a man like this in whom God's spirit lives?" Pharaoh said to Joseph "Since God has taught you all this there is no one so keen and wise as you. You shall be over my house and all my people shall yield to your mouth. Only with regard to the throne will I be greater than you." Pharaoh said to Joseph "See, I have put you over all Egypt" and Pharaoh took his signet from his hand and put it on Joseph's hand, dressed him in clothes of fine linen, put a gold chain round his neck and made him ride in his second chariot—they shouted "*Abrek*" before him. So he put him over all Egypt and then Pharaoh said to Joseph "I am Pharaoh and without you a man shall not lift hand or foot in all Egypt." Pharaoh called Joseph by the name Zaphenath-

paneah and gave him as a wife Asenath daughter of
Potiphera, priest of On, and Joseph rose over Egypt.

Joseph was thirty years old when he stood before
Pharaoh king of Egypt. When Joseph left Pharaoh he
passed through all Egypt. In the seven years of plenty
the land produced by handfuls. He saved all the food
from the seven years in Egypt and put the food in the
cities—in the midst of each city he put the food of the
fields round it. Joseph piled grain like sea sand
enormously till he stopped counting as there was no
number and before the year of the famine came in two
sons were born to Joseph whom Asenath daughter of
Potiphera, priest of On, bore him. Joseph called the
firstborn by the name Manasseh for "God has made
me forget all my labor and all my father's house." He
called the second by the name Ephraim for "God has
made me fruitful in the land of my sorrow."

The seven years of plenty in Egypt ended and the
seven years of famine began to come in as Joseph had
said and there was famine in all lands but everywhere
in Egypt there was bread.

When all Egypt also hungered and the people
cried to Pharaoh for bread, Pharaoh said to all Egypt
"Go to Joseph. What he says to you, do." Famine was
on the whole face of the land and Joseph opened what
there was and rationed to the Egyptians since famine
was bad in Egypt. Then the whole earth came to Egypt
to Joseph to buy since famine was bad in the whole
earth.

When Jacob saw there was grain in Egypt, Jacob
said to his sons "Why stare at each other?" He said
"Look, I've heard there is grain in Egypt. Go down

there and buy for us so we may live and not die." So Joseph's ten brothers went down to buy grain from Egypt but Jacob did not send Benjamin, Joseph's whole-brother, with his brothers because he said "Harm may come to him."

Israel's sons came to buy among the others coming since famine was in Canaan too and—since Joseph was governor of the land, the one selling to all the earth's people—Joseph's brothers came in and bowed down to him face to the earth.

Joseph saw his brothers and recognized them but made himself strange to them and said stern things to them. He said to them "Where have you come from?"

They said "From Canaan to buy food."

When Joseph recognized his brothers and they did not recognize him he remembered the dreams he had dreamed about them and said to them "You're spies. You've come to see the land's nakedness."

They said to him "No, my lord. Your servants have come to buy food. We're all sons of one man. We're honest. Your servants have not been spies."

He said to them "No. You've come to see the land's nakedness."

They said "We your servants are twelve brothers, sons of one man in Canaan. Look, the youngest is with our father today and another one is gone."

Joseph said to them "That's what I told you— you're spies. You'll be tested by this—you shall not leave here as Pharaoh lives unless your youngest brother comes here. So send one of you and let him get your brother while the rest of you be captive and let your words be tested whether the truth is in you or sure as

Pharaoh lives you're spies." He put them together into custody three days. On the third day Joseph said to them "Do this and live—I fear God. If you're honest let one of your brothers be captive in your prison and you go and take grain for the famine in your houses. Bring your youngest brother to me and let your words be seconded and you shall not die."

They agreed and each said to his brother "Truly we are guilty because of our brother since we saw his soul's anguish when he begged us and didn't hear him. So this anguish has come upon us."

Reuben answered them by saying "Didn't I tell you 'Don't sin against the boy' and you didn't listen? Look, his blood is demanded."

They did not know that Joseph understood since an interpreter was between them.

He turned away from them and wept. Then when he could speak to them again he took Simeon from them and bound him before their eyes. Then Joseph commanded to fill their containers with grain, to put back each man's money in his sack and to give them rations for the road.

It was done for them.

They loaded their grain on their asses and left and when one opened his sack to give his ass fodder in the camp he saw his money—look, it was in the mouth of his bag. He said to his brothers "My money has been returned—look, in my bag."

Their heart fell and they were terrified each saying to his brother "What has God done to us?"

They came to Jacob their father in Canaan and told him all the things that had happened to them saying "The man, the lord of the land, spoke harsh things to us and thought us spies on the land. We said to him 'We're honest. We have not been spies. We're twelve brothers, sons of our father—one is gone and the youngest is with our father today in Canaan.' The man, the lord of the land, said to us 'By this I'll know you're honest—leave one of your brothers with me, take rations for the famine in your houses and go. Bring your youngest brother to me so I may know you're not spies and are honest. Then I will give you your brother and you may wander round the land." It happened as they were emptying their sacks—look, in each one's sack was his moneybag. They and their father were afraid.

Jacob their father said to them "You have stripped me. Joseph is gone, Simeon is gone, now you'll take Benjamin. All these things are against me."

Reuben said to his father "You may kill my two sons if I don't bring him to you. Put him into my hand and I'll return him to you."

He said "My son shall not go down with you for his brother is dead and only he is left. If harm came to him on the way you go you would send my white head in sorrow down to Sheol."

The famine was hard in the land so—it happened when they finished eating the grain they had brought from Egypt—their father said to them "Go back and buy a little food for us."

Judah said to him "The man protested strongly to us and said 'You shall not see my face unless your brother is with you.' If you're sending our brother with us we'll go down and buy you food. If you aren't sending him we won't go down since the man said to us 'You shall not see my face unless your brother is with you.' "

Israel said "Why do you do me wrong?—to tell the man whether there was another brother."

They said "The man asked again and again about us and our kin saying 'Is your father still alive? Do you have a brother?' We told him what we had to. Could we really know he'd say 'Bring your brother down'?"

Judah said to Israel his father "Send the boy with me and we'll rise and go so we live and do not die, we and you and our children. I will be bond for him— demand him from my hand. If I don't bring him to you and put him before you I'll be a sinner against you always. If we hadn't delayed by now we'd have returned here twice."

Israel their father said to them "If it must be do this then—take some of the land's best produce in your baggage and carry a present down to the man: a little balsam, a little honey, gum, ladanum, pistachios and almonds. Take double money in hand and in hand return the money put back in the mouth of your bags— it may have been an error. Now take your brother and set out for the man and may El Shaddai give you mercy before the man so he send away your other brother and Benjamin. If I'm stripped I'm stripped."

The men took the gift, took double money in their hand and Benjamin, set out for Egypt and stood before Joseph.

Joseph saw them with Benjamin and said to the man in charge of his house "Bring the men to the house, kill and dress an animal for the men shall eat with me at noon."

The man did as Joseph said. Then the man brought the men to Joseph's house.

The men were afraid at being brought to Joseph's house. They said "Because of the money put back in our bags last time, we're brought here—to roll down on us, fall on us and take us and our asses for slaves." So they came up to the man in charge of Joseph's house and spoke to him at the door of the house. They said "O my lord, we really did come down to buy food last time but it happened when we got into camp and opened our bags—look, each one's money in the mouth of his bag, our money in full weight. We've brought down other money in hand to buy food. We don't know who put our money in our bags."

He said "Peace to you. Don't fear. Your God and your father's God put treasure in your bags. I got your money." He brought Simeon out to them. The man brought the men to Joseph's house, gave them water and they washed their feet. He gave them fodder for their asses.

They prepared the gift for Joseph's arrival at noon since they had heard they should eat bread there. When Joseph came into the house they brought him the gift in their hand into the house and bowed themselves to the earth to him.

He asked them about their welfare and said "Is your father at peace, the old man of whom you spoke? Is he still alive?"

They said "At peace—your servant our father. He's still alive." They bowed most humbly.

He raised his eyes, saw his brother Benjamin (his mother's son) and said "Is this your youngest brother of whom you spoke to me?" He said "God be gracious

to you, my son." Then Joseph hurried for his feelings
were stirred toward his brother and he needed to weep.
He went to an inner room and wept there. Then he
washed his face, went out and controlled himself and
said "Serve bread."

They served him by himself, them by themselves
and the Egyptians eating with him by themselves since
Egyptians cannot eat bread with Hebrews (it is an
abomination in Egypt). They sat at his order—the
firstborn by his birthright and the youngest by his
youth—and the men were amazed each to his neighbor.
He sent them portions from his own.

Benjamin's portion was five times larger than the
portions of all.

They feasted and were drunk with him.

He commanded the man in charge of his house by
saying "Fill the men's bags with food as much as they
can carry and put each one's money in the mouth of his
bag. My cup, the silver cup—put that in the mouth of
the youngest's bag with his grain money."

He did what Joseph said.

At first light the men were sent off, they and their
asses.

When they were not far gone from the city Joseph
said to the men in charge of his house "Up! Run after
the men. Catch them and say to them 'Why have you
repaid evil for good? Isn't this the one from which my
lord always drinks, in which he actually takes omens?
What you've done is evil.' "

He overtook them and said those words.

They said to him "Why should my lord say such
words? Far be it from your servants to do what you've
said. Look, the money we found in the mouth of our

bags we brought back to you from Canaan. Then how could we steal silver or gold from your lord's house? With whichever of your servants it's found he shall die and we also will be slaves to my lord."

He said "Well now as you said so let it be with whichever it's found on—he'll be a slave to me and you shall be innocent."

They hurried, each one brought his bag down to the ground and each one opened his bag.

He searched starting with the eldest and ending with the youngest. The cup was found in Benjamin's bag.

They tore their clothes and each one loaded his ass and returned to the city. Judah and his brothers entered Joseph's house—he was still there—and fell to the ground before him.

Joseph said to them "What deed is this you've done? Surely you knew a man like me would take omens?"

Judah said "What can we say to my lord? How can we beg? What way can we justify ourselves? God has discovered your servants' wrong. Look, we're slaves to my lord, both we and he in whose hand the cup was found."

He said "Far be it from me to do this. The man in whose hand the cup was found shall be a slave to me but the rest of you go up to your father in peace."

Then Judah came near him and said "O my lord, let your servant please speak a word in my lord's ears and don't let your anger burn against your servant for you are like Pharaoh. My lord asked his servants 'Do you have a father or a brother?' and we said to my lord 'We have a father, an old man, and a child of his old age—a young one. His brother is dead and he alone is left of his mother and his father loves him.' And you said to your servants 'Bring him down to me and let me set my eye on him.' We said to my lord 'The boy can't leave his father. If he should leave his father he'd die.' And you said to your servants 'If your youngest brother doesn't come down with you you shall not go on seeing my face.' It happened when we'd gone up to your servant my father and told him my lord's words our father said 'Go back. Buy us a little food' and we said 'We can't go down. If our youngest brother is with us then we'll go down since we can't see this man's face unless our youngest brother is with us.' Your servant my father said to us 'You know my wife bore me two sons. One left me and I said "Oh surely he's torn to pieces" and I haven't seen him till now. If you also take this one from before my face and harm comes to him you'll send my gray head in sorrow to Sheol.' So now when I come to your servant my father and the boy is not with us (his soul being tied to his soul) it shall happen when he sees the boy is not with us—he'll die. Your servants shall bring down the gray head of your servant our father in grief to Sheol. For your servant was bond for the boy with my father saying 'If I don't bring him to you I'll bear the blame to my father always.' Now then please let your servant stay instead of the boy—a slave to my lord. Let the boy go up with his brothers. How can I go up to my father, the boy not with me? Then I'd see the evil that would take my father."

Joseph could not restrain himself before those standing near him. He cried "Make everyone leave me." So no one stood with him when Joseph made himself known to his brothers but he wept aloud and

the Egyptians heard and so Pharaoh's house heard.
Joseph said to his brothers "I am Joseph. Is my father
still alive?"

His brothers could not answer for they were
frightened at his presence.

Joseph said to his brothers "Come near me now."
They came near.

And he said "I'm your brother whom you sold into
Egypt. Don't be grieved and show no anger in your
eyes that you sold me here—God sent me before you to
save life. For two years now famine has been in the
land and five more shall come with no plowing and
harvest. God sent me before you to save you a remnant
on earth and to save your lives by a great deliverance.
So it was not you but God who sent me here and He
has set me up as father to Pharaoh, lord of all his house
and ruler of all Egypt. Hurry and go up to my father
and say to him 'Joseph your son says this "God has set
me up as lord of all Egypt. Come down to me and
don't delay. You shall live in Goshen and be near me—
you and your sons, your sons' sons, your flocks and
herds and all you own. I'll nourish you there—there are
still five years of famine—so you are not ruined, you
and your household and all you own." ' Look, your eyes
are seeing and my brother Benjamin's eyes that my own
mouth is speaking to you! Tell my father all my honors
in Egypt and all you've seen. But hurry and bring my
father down here." He fell on the neck of his brother
Benjamin and wept.

Benjamin wept on his neck.

Then he kissed all his brothers and wept on them.
And afterward his brothers talked with him.

The news was heard in Pharaoh's house saying

"Joseph's brothers have come"—it was pleasing in the eyes of Pharaoh and his servants.

Pharaoh said to Joseph "Say to your brothers 'Do this—load your animals and leave, go to Canaan, get your father and your households and come to me. I'll give you the good land of Egypt. You'll eat the fat of the land. You are commanded—do this: take yourselves wagons from Egypt for your children and wives. Bring your father and come. Don't let your eye linger on your belongings—the good land of all Egypt is yours.

Israel's sons did so.

Joseph gave them wagons on the order of Pharaoh and provisions for the trip. To all of them he gave, each man, changes of clothes but to Benjamin he gave three hundred pieces of silver and five changes of clothes. To his father he sent this—ten asses bearing Egypt's good things and ten she-asses bearing grain, bread and other food for his father for the trip. Then he sent his brothers off.

And they left.

But he said to them "Don't quarrel on the way."

They went up from Egypt and came to Canaan to Jacob their father and told him "Joseph is still alive and is ruler of all Egypt."

His heart chilled for he did not believe them.

So they told him all the words Joseph told them.

Then he saw the wagons Joseph had sent to bear him and the spirit of their father Jacob revived. Israel said "Enough!—Joseph my son is still alive. I'll go and see him before I die."

Israel left with all he had, came to Beersheba and sacrificed to the God of his father Isaac.

God spoke to Israel in visions at night. He said "Jacob, Jacob." And He said "I am El your father's God. Do not fear going down to Egypt since I will make you a great nation there. I will go down to Egypt with you and I will surely bring you up again and Joseph's hand shall shut your eyes."

Jacob rose from Beersheba and Israel's sons took their father Jacob, their children and wives in the wagons Pharaoh had sent to carry him. They took their cattle, the belongings they had got in Canaan and they entered Egypt—Jacob and all his seed with him. His sons and his sons' sons, his daughters and his sons' daughters and all his seed he brought with him to Egypt.

These are the names of Israel's sons who came to Egypt, Jacob and his sons—Jacob's firstborn Reuben and Reuben's sons: Hanoch, Pallu, Hezron and Carmi. Simeon's sons: Jemuel, Jamin, Ohad, Jachin, Zohar and Shaul the son of a Canaanite woman. Levi's sons: Gershon, Kohath and Merari. Judah's sons: Er, Onan, Shelah, Perez and Zerah (Er and Onan died in Canaan). Perez' sons were Hezron and Hamul; Issachar's sons: Tola, Puvah, Iob and Shimron. Zebulun's sons: Sered, Elon and Jahleel (these were Leah's sons whom she bore Jacob in Paddan-aram along with his daughter Dinah). All the souls of his sons and daughters were thirty-three. Gad's sons: Ziphion, Haggi, Shuni, Ezbon, Eri, Arodi and Areli. Asher's sons: Imnah, Ishvah, Ishvi, Beriah and Serah their sister. Beriah's sons: Heber and Malchiel (these were the sons of Zilpah whom Laban gave to Leah his daughter and she bore these to Jacob—sixteen souls). The sons of Jacob's wife Rachel: Joseph and Benjamin.

Manasseh and Ephraim were born to Joseph in Egypt whom Asenath daughter of Potiphera, priest of On, bore him. Benjamin's sons: Bela, Becher, Ashbel, Gera, Naaman, Ehi, Rosh, Muppim, Huppim and Ard (these were Rachel's sons born to Jacob, fourteen souls in all). Dan's sons: Hushim. Naphtali's sons: Jahzeel, Guni, Jezer and Shillem (these were sons of Bilhah whom Laban gave to his daughter Rachel, born to Jacob— seven souls in all). All the souls coming into Egypt with Jacob, those proceeding from his loins besides the wives of Jacob's sons—the souls were sixty-six and Joseph's sons born to him in Egypt were two souls. So all the souls from Jacob's household entering Egypt were seventy.

He sent Judah before him to Joseph to meet him in Goshen.

Joseph hitched his chariot, went up to Goshen to meet his father Israel and appeared before him. He fell on his neck and wept long on his neck.

Israel said to Joseph "Let me die now after seeing your face—you're still alive."

Joseph said to his brothers and his father's household "I'll go up and tell Pharaoh. I'll say to him 'My brothers and my father's household who were in Canaan have come to me. The men are shepherds for they've always been stockmen and they've brought their flocks, their herds, their all.' It shall happen when Pharaoh calls you and says 'What's your work?' you'll say 'Your servants have been stockmen from our youth till now, both we and our fathers' so you may stay in Goshen since any shepherd is the horror of Egypt."

Joseph went in and told Pharaoh "My father, my brothers, their flocks and herds and all their belongings

have come from Canaan. Look, they're in Goshen."
From among his brothers he took five men and stood
them before Pharaoh.

Pharaoh said to his brothers "What's your work?"

They said to Pharaoh "Your servants are shepherds,
both we and our fathers." Then they said to Pharaoh
"We've come to live in this land since there's no
grazing your servants' flocks with the famine heavy in
Canaan. Now please let your servants stay in Goshen."

Pharaoh said to Joseph "Your father and brothers
have come to you. Egypt is before you. Let your father
and brothers stay in the best land—let them stay in
Goshen. And if you know any able men among them
make them foremen over my stock."

So Joseph brought in Jacob his father and set him
before Pharaoh.

Jacob greeted Pharaoh.

Then Pharaoh said to Jacob "How many are the
days of the years of your life?"

Jacob said to Pharaoh "The days of the years of
my stay are a hundred and thirty years. Few and hard
have been the days of the years of my life. They haven't
reached the days of the years of the life of my fathers in
the days of their stay." Jacob blessed Pharaoh and went
out from before him.

Joseph settled his father and brothers, gave them
belongings in Egypt—the best land in the district of
Rameses as Pharaoh ordered—and Joseph fed his
father, brothers and all his father's household with
bread in respect to the mouths of their children.

THE GOOD NEWS ACCORDING TO MARK

BEGINNING OF THE GOOD NEWS OF JESUS MESSIAH

As it was written in Isaiah the prophet

"Look, I send My messenger before your face
Who shall prepare your way,
Voice of one crying in the desert
'Prepare the Lord's way,
Make his paths straight.' "

John the Baptizer came into the desert proclaiming baptism of repentance for pardon of sins.

All the country of Judea went out to him and those from Jerusalem and were baptized by him in the Jordan river confessing their sins.

John wore camel's hair and a leather belt round his hips, ate grasshoppers and wild honey and proclaimed saying "He's coming who is stronger than I—after me—of whom I'm unfit stooping to loosen the strap of his sandals. I baptized you in water but he'll baptize you in Holy Spirit."

It happened in those days—Jesus came from Nazareth in Galilee and was baptized in the Jordan by John. At once going up out of the water he saw the sky torn open and the Spirit like a dove descending to him.

There was a voice out of the sky "You are My son, the loved one. In you I have delighted."

At once the Spirit drove him into the desert. He was in the desert forty days tempted by Satan and was with wild beasts.

The angels served him.

After John was handed over Jesus came into Galilee proclaiming God's good news and saying "The time has ripened and the reign of God has approached. Turn and believe the good news." Passing by the sea of Galilee he saw Simon and Andrew, Simon's brother, casting a net into the sea (they were fishermen) and Jesus said to them "Come after me and I'll make you fishers for men."

At once leaving the nets they followed him.

Going on a little he saw James—Zebedee's James—and John his brother right in the boat mending nets. At once he called them and leaving their father Zebedee in the boat with the hands they went after him.

They went into Capernaum and at once on the sabbath entering the synagogue he taught.

They were amazed at his teaching for he was teaching them as if he had the right and not like the scholars.

At once there was in their synagogue a man with a foul spirit and he screamed saying "What are you to us, Jesus Nazarene? Did you come to destroy us? I know you for what you are—the Holy One of God!"

Jesus warned him saying "Silence! Come out of him."

Tearing him the foul spirit cried in a loud voice and came out of him.

All were stunned so they debated among themselves saying "What is this?—a new teaching by right? He commands the foul spirits and they obey him." Word of him went out at once everywhere all round the country of Galilee.

Going out of the synagogue at once they came to Simon and Andrew's house with James and John. Simon's mother-in-law was laid up with fever and at once they told him about her.

Approaching he raised her holding her hand.

The fever left her so she served them.

Then when dusk came and the sun set they brought him all the sick and the demoniac. The whole city was gathered at the door.

He cured many who were sick with various diseases and expelled many demons and did not let the demons speak because they knew him.

And very early—still night—he rose and went out and left for a lonely place and prayed there.

Simon and those with him tracked him down, found him and said to him "Everyone's looking for you."

He said to them "Let's go elsewhere to the nearest towns so I may preach there too. I came for this." And he preached in their synagogues in all Galilee and expelled demons.

A leper came to him begging him, kneeling and saying to him "If you will you can cleanse me."

Filled with pity, stretching out his hand, he touched him and said "I will. Be clean."

At once the leprosy left him and he was clean.

Then warning him sternly he ran him off and said to him "Say nothing—to no one—but go show yourself to the priest and offer for your cleansing what Moses ordered as testimony to them."

But he going off began to declare many things and spread the word.

So he could no longer enter a city openly but was out in desert places.

And they came to him from everywhere.

When he entered Capernaum again after days it was heard he was at home and many gathered so there was no room not even at the door and he spoke the word to them.

They came to him bringing a cripple borne by four men and unable to reach him because of the crowd they tore off the roof where he was and having broken in they lowered the pallet on which the cripple was lying.

Seeing their faith Jesus said to the cripple "Son, your sins are forgiven you."

But there were some scholars sitting there debating in their hearts "Why does this man speak thus? He blasphemes. Who can forgive sins but one—God?"

At once Jesus knowing in his soul that they were debating thus among themselves said to them "Why do you debate these things in your hearts? What is easier?—to say to the cripple 'Your sins are forgiven' or to say 'Stand. Take your pallet and walk'? But so you know the Son of Man has the right to forgive sins on earth" he said to the cripple "To you I say stand, take your pallet and go home."

He stood and at once taking the pallet went out in sight of all so that all were astonished and praised God saying "We never saw the like."

He went out again by the sea and all the crowd

came to him and he taught them. And walking along he saw Levi—Alpheus' Levi—sitting at the tax office and said to him "Follow me."

Standing he followed him.

Then it happened as he lay at table in his house—many tax collectors and sinners lay back with Jesus and his disciples for there were many and they followed him.

The Pharisee scholars seeing him eating with sinners and tax collectors said to his disciples "Does he eat with sinners and tax collectors?"

Hearing Jesus said to them "The strong don't need a doctor but the sick do. I came not to call just men but sinners."

Now John's disciples and the Pharisees were fasting and they came and said to him "Why do John's disciples and the Pharisees' disciples fast but your disciples don't fast?"

Jesus said to them "Can the sons of the bridal-chamber fast while the bridegroom is with them? The time they have the bridegroom with them they can't fast. But days shall come when the bridegroom shall be taken from them and then on that day they'll fast. No one sews a patch of unshrunk cloth on old clothes otherwise the new pulls on the old and a worse tear starts. And no one puts new wine into old skins or the new wine splits the skins and the wine is lost and the skins. No, new wine is put in fresh skins."

Then this happened as he was walking on the sabbath through the grainfields and his disciples as they made a path began pulling stalks.

The Pharisees said to him "Look, why do they do on the sabbath what's not right?"

He said to them "Didn't you ever read what David

did when he was needy and hungered?—he and those with him—how he entered God's house in the time of Highpriest Abiathar and ate the presentation loaves which it's not right to eat except for priests and also gave to those with him?" And he said to them "The sabbath was made because of man not man because of the sabbath. So the Son of Man is also lord of the sabbath."

He entered the synagogue again and there was a man who had a withered hand.

They were watching him closely whether on the sabbath he would heal him so they might charge him.

He said to the man who had the withered hand "Stand in the middle here." And he said to them "Is it right on the sabbath to do good or to do evil, to save life or kill?"

But they were silent.

Looking round at them with anger, grieved at the hardness of their heart he said to the man "Stretch out the hand."

He stretched it out and his hand was restored.

Leaving the Pharisees at once consulted with the Herodians against him so they might destroy him.

Jesus withdrew with his disciples to the sea.

And a great throng from Galilee followed him and from Judea, from Jerusalem, from Idumea, from beyond the Jordan and round Tyre and Sidon a great throng hearing what he did came to him.

He told his disciples that a little boat should wait near him because of the crowd so they might not rush him for he healed many so that they fell on him to touch him as many as had torments. And the foul spirits when they saw him fell down before him and cried saying "You're the Son of God."

He warned them strictly that they not reveal him.

And he climbed the mountain and called to him the ones he wanted.

They went to him.

He appointed twelve to be with him to send out to preach and to have the right to expel demons. He gave Simon the name Peter. And Zebedee's James and John, James's brother—he gave them the name *Boanerges* which is "Sons of Thunder"—and Andrew, Philip, Bartholomew, Matthew, Thomas, Alpheus' James, Thaddeus, Simon the Cananean and Judas Iscariot who also handed him over.

He came into a house and again a crowd gathered so they could not even eat bread.

Hearing his family went out to seize him for they said "He's beside himself."

And the scholars who came down from Jerusalem said "He has Beelzebul and by the prince of demons he expels demons."

Calling them to him in parables he said "How can Satan expel Satan? And if a kingdom is divided against itself that kingdom can't stand and if a house is divided against itself that house can't stand. And if Satan stood against himself and were divided he couldn't stand but would end. No man can—entering the house of the Strong Man—plunder his goods unless he binds the Strong Man first. Then he shall plunder his house. Amen I say to you that all shall be forgiven the sons of men— sins and whatever blasphemies they may blaspheme —but whoever blasphemes against the Holy Spirit has no forgiveness to eternity but is subject to eternal sin because they said 'He has a foul spirit.' "

His mother and his brothers came and standing outside sent to him calling him.

A crowd sat round him and said to him "Look, your mother and your brothers outside seek you."

Answering them he said "Who is my mother and my brothers?" and looking round at the ones sitting round him in a ring he said "Look, my mother and my brothers. Whoever does God's will—that one is my brother, sister and mother."

Again he began to teach by the sea and a great crowd gathered to him so that climbing into a boat he sat on the sea and all the crowd was on land close to the sea. He taught them much in parables and said to them in his teaching "Listen. Look, the sower went out to sow and it happened as he sowed—some fell by the road and birds came and ate it up. Another part fell on the rocky place where there wasn't much earth and at once it sprouted because it had no depth of earth and when the sun rose it was burnt and because of not having root it withered. Another part fell into thorns and the thorns grew up and choked it and it bore no fruit. Another part fell into good ground and bore fruit growing up and increasing and bore in thirties, sixties and hundreds." Then he said to them "Who has ears to hear let him hear."

When he was alone those round him with the twelve asked him about the parables.

He said to them "The mystery of the reign of God has been given to you but to those outside everything is in parables so

Seeing they may see and not find
　　And hearing they may hear and not understand—
Otherwise they'd turn and be forgiven."

And he said to them "Don't you know this parable? Then how will you know all the parables? The sower sows the word and these are the ones by the road where the word is sown and when they hear at once Satan comes and takes away the word sown in them. These are likewise the ones sown in rocky places who when they hear the word at once accept it with joy and have no root in themselves but are temporary. Then trouble or persecution coming because of the word at once they are made to fall. Others are the ones sown among thorns. These are the ones hearing the word and—the cares of the time, the cheat of riches and the other passions entering choke the word and it becomes barren. And those are the ones sown in good ground who hear the word and welcome it and bear fruit in thirties, sixties and hundreds." And he said to them "Does the lamp come so it can be put under the measuring bowl or under the couch?—not so it can be put on the lampstand? For nothing is hidden that shall not be shown or veiled except it come into the open. If any has ears to hear let him hear." And he said to them "Take care what you hear—with whatever measure you measure it shall be measured to you and added to you for, whoever has, to him shall be given and, who has not, even what he has shall be taken from him." And he said "Such is the reign of God—as if a man should throw seed on the ground and should sleep and rise night and day and the seed should sprout and lengthen he doesn't know how: on her own the earth yields fruit, first a blade then an ear then full grain in the ear. And when the fruit offers itself at once he puts in the sickle for the harvest has come." And he said "To what can we liken the reign of God? Or in what parable could we put it?—like a grain of mustard which when it's sown on the ground is smaller than all seeds on the ground but when it's sown grows up and becomes greater than all plants and makes big branches so the birds of the air can live under its shadow." In many such parables he spoke the word to them as far as they could hear it but without a parable he never spoke to them though aside to his own disciples he explained everything.

He said to them on that day when evening had come "Let's cross over to the other side" and dismissing the crowd they took him just as he was in the boat and other boats were with him. A violent windstorm came and waves poured into the boat so that it was now full. He was in the stern on a pillow sleeping.

They woke him and said to him "Teacher, it's nothing to you that we're perishing?"

Awake he warned the wind and said to the sea "Silence. Be still."

The wind fell and there was great calm.

He said to them "Why be so cowardly? Where is your faith?"

They feared with great dread and said to each other "Who is this then that even the wind and sea obey him?"

They came to the far side of the sea to Gerasene country. When he got out of the boat at once a man from the tombs with a foul spirit met him—his home was in the tombs. Even with a chain no one could bind him since he had often been bound with shackles and chains and the chains had been broken by him, the shackles had been smashed and no one was able to tame him. Always night and day in the tombs and mountains he was screaming and slashing himself with rocks. Seeing Jesus from a distance he ran and worshipped him and screaming in a loud voice he said

"What am I to you, Jesus Son of the Highest God? I beg you by God don't torture me" for he had been saying to him "Out, foul spirit. Out of the man."

He asked him "What is your name?"

He said to him "Legion is my name because we are many" and he pled hard with Jesus not to send them out of the country. Now there was there close to the mountain a big herd of pigs feeding and all the demons pled saying "Send us to the pigs so we can enter them."

He let them.

Going out the foul spirits entered the pigs and the herd rushed down a cliff into the sea—there were about two thousand—and were choked in the sea.

The ones herding them fled and reported it to the town and the villages and they came out to see what it was that had happened. They came to Jesus and saw the demoniac sitting dressed and in his right mind— him who had had the Legion—and they were afraid. Those who had seen how it happened to the demoniac told them and about the pigs so they began to plead with him to leave their district.

As he boarded the boat the demoniac pled to be with him.

He did not let him but said to him "Go to your home to your people and report to them how much the Lord has done for you and pitied you."

He left and began to spread word through Decapolis how much Jesus did for him.

All men wondered.

When Jesus had crossed in the boat again to the far side a great crowd swarmed to him—he was by the sea—and one of the synagogue leaders named Jairus came and seeing him fell at his feet and pled hard saying "My little daughter is at the point of death. Come and lay your hands on her so she may be cured and live."

He went with him.

And a great crowd followed him and pressed round him.

Then a woman who had had a flow of blood twelve years and had suffered many things from many doctors and had spent all she owned and gained nothing but rather grown worse, hearing things about Jesus came up behind in the crowd and touched his coat saying "If I can touch just his clothes I'll be healed" and at once the fountain of her blood was dried and she knew in her body that she was cured from the scourge.

At once Jesus knowing in himself that his streaming power had gone out of him turned to the crowd and said "Who touched my clothes?"

His disciples said to him "You see the crowd pressing round you and you say 'Who touched me?' "

He looked round to see her who had done this.

So the woman—dreading and shaking, knowing what had happened to her—came and fell before him and told him all the truth.

He said to her "Daughter, your faith has cured you. Go in peace and be well of your scourge."

While he was still speaking they came from the synagogue leader's saying "Your daughter died. Why bother the teacher still?"

But Jesus ignoring the word just spoken said to the synagogue leader "Don't fear. Only believe" and he let no one go with him but Peter, James and John (James's brother).

They came to the house of the synagogue leader. He saw a commotion, people weeping and wailing hard. Entering he said to them "Why make a commotion and weep? The child is not dead but sleeps."

They mocked him.

But expelling them all he took the child's father, mother and those with him and went in where the child was. Grasping the child's hand he said to her *"Talitha koum"* which is translated "Little girl, I tell you rise."

At once the little girl stood and walked round— she was twelve years old—and at once they were astonished with great wildness.

He ordered them strictly that no one should know this and told them to give her something to eat.

He went out of there and came to his own town and his disciples followed him. When a sabbath came he began to teach in the synagogue.

Many hearing were amazed saying "From where did all these things come to this man and what is the wisdom given to him that such acts of power are done through his hands? Isn't this man the carpenter, the son of Mary and brother of James and Joses and Judas and Simon and aren't his sisters here with us?" They were offended by him.

Jesus said to them "A prophet is not dishonored except in his own town and among his kin and in his own house" and he could not do there any act of power except to a few sick—laying hands on them, he healed. He wondered at their doubting.

And he toured the villages round there teaching. He called the twelve to him and began to send them out two by two and gave them rights over foul spirits and ordered them to take nothing for the road except one stick—no bread, no wallet, no money in the belt—but be shod with sandals and not wear two shirts. He said to them "Wherever you enter a house stay there till you leave there and whatever place will not receive you or hear you, leaving there shake off the dust under your feet as a witness to them."

Going out they proclaimed that men should change. They expelled many demons, anointed many of the sick with oil and healed them.

King Herod heard—his name became widespread and they were saying "John the Baptizer has been raised from the dead which is why acts of power work through him" but others said "It's Elijah" and still others said "A prophet like one of the prophets." But hearing Herod said "The one I beheaded—John: he was raised" for Herod himself had sent and arrested John and bound him in prison because of Herodias the wife of Philip his brother since he had married her. For John said to Herod "It's not right for you to have your brother's wife." So Herodias had a grudge against him and wanted to kill him but could not for Herod feared John knowing him a just and holy man and protected him and hearing him was shaken but gladly heard him. Then when a suitable day came Herod gave a supper on his birthday for his great men and the tribunes and leading men of Galilee. The daughter of Herodias herself entered and dancing pleased Herod and those lying back with him. So the king said to the girl "Ask me whatever you want and I'll give it to you" and he swore to her "Whatever you ask I'll give you up to half my kingdom." Going out she said to her mother "What must I ask?" She said "The head of John the Baptizer."

At once entering eagerly to the king she asked saying "I want you to give me right now on a dish the head of John the Baptist." The king, anguished because of the oaths and those lying back with him, did not want to refuse her so at once sending an executioner the king commanded his head to be brought. Going he beheaded him in the prison, brought his head on a dish, gave it to the girl and the girl gave it to her mother. Hearing his disciples went, took his corpse and put it in a tomb.

And the apostles gathered back to Jesus and told him all they had done and taught.

He said to them "Come away by yourselves alone to a lonely place and rest a little" since those coming and going were many and they had no chance even to eat. They went off in the boat to a lonely place alone.

Many saw them going, knew and on foot from all the cities ran there together and preceded them.

Going out he saw a great crowd, pitied them since they were like sheep having no shepherd and began to teach them many things.

When it was late the disciples approached him and said "The place is lonely and it's late. Dismiss them so that going off to the neighboring farms and villages they can buy themselves something to eat."

But answering he said to them "You give them something to eat."

They said to him "Shall we go off and buy two hundred denarii-worth of loaves and give them to eat?"

He said to them "How many loaves do you have? Go see."

Knowing they said "Five and two fish."

He told them to lie back in parties on the green grass.

They lay back in groups by hundreds and fifties.

Then taking the five loaves and two fish, looking up to heaven he blessed and broke the loaves, gave them to the disciples to set before them and the two fish he spread among all.

All ate and were fed and they took up twelve full baskets of crumbs and fish. Those eating the loaves were five thousand men.

At once he made his disciples board the boat and go ahead to the far side of Bethsaida until he dismissed the crowd. And saying goodbye to them he went off to the mountain to pray.

When dusk came on the boat was in the middle of the sea and he alone on land and seeing them straining at the rowing for the wind was against them about three o'clock in the night he came toward them walking on the sea and wanted to pass them.

But seeing him walking on the sea they thought it was a ghost and cried out—all saw him and were frightened.

But at once he spoke with them and said "Courage. I am. No fear." And he went up to them into the boat and the wind dropped.

In themselves they were deeply astonished since they did not understand about the loaves as their heart was hardened.

Crossing over to land they came to Gennesaret and anchored.

When they came out of the ship at once knowing him they ran round all the countryside and began to haul the sick round on pallets where they heard he was and wherever he entered villages or cities or farms they put the sick in marketplaces and begged him to touch even the hem of his coat and as many as touched him were healed.

The Pharisees gathered to him and some of the scholars from Jerusalem and seeing some of his disciples eating bread with dirty hands—that is, not washed (for the Pharisees and all the Jews do not eat unless they scrub their hands, keeping the way of the elders, and coming from markets they do not eat unless they rinse and there are many other things which they have accepted to keep: washing cups, pitchers and kettles)— the Pharisees and scholars questioned him "Why don't your disciples walk after the way of the elders but eat bread with dirty hands?"

He said to them "Isaiah prophesied rightly about you hypocrites since it is written

'This people honors Me with lips
But their heart is far from Me.
They worship Me in vain,
Teaching teachings which are men's commands.'

Deserting God's command you keep man's way." And he said to them "Rightly you put aside God's command so you may keep your way for Moses said *'Honor your father and your mother'* and *'He who reviles father or mother let him die.'* But you say if a man says to his father 'Whatever you might have got from me is *Korban'* " (that is, a gift) "then you no longer let him do anything for his father or mother, canceling God's word in the way you've accepted. You do many such things."

Calling the crowd to him again he said "Hear me all of you and understand. There is nothing outside a man that entering him can defile him but the things coming out of a man are the things that defile him. If anyone has ears to hear let him hear."

When he entered a house from the crowd his disciples questioned him about the parable. He said to them "Then you too are stupid? Don't you understand that anything outside entering a man can't defile him because it doesn't enter his heart but his belly and goes into the privy purging all foods?" He said "The thing coming out of a man defiles a man. For from inside out of the heart of man bad thoughts come—fornications, thefts, murders, adulteries, greeds, malice, deceits, lust, evil eye, slander, pride, folly: all these evil things come from inside and defile a man."

Rising from there he went off to the district of Tyre. When he entered a house he wanted no one to know but he could not be hid.

At once a woman whose young daughter had a foul spirit heard of him and coming fell at his feet. The woman was a Greek, a Syro-Phoenician by race, and she asked him to expel the demon from her daughter.

He said to her "Let the children be fed first. It's not right to take the children's bread and throw it to pups."

She answered and said to him "Yes sir but pups under the table eat the children's crumbs."

He said to her "For that saying go. The demon has gone out of your daughter."

And going away to her house she found the child laid on the couch and the demon gone.

Going out again from the district of Tyre he came through Sidon to the sea of Galilee in the middle of the district of Decapolis. And they brought him a deaf man with a stammer and they begged him to put his hand on him. Taking him apart from the crowd he put his fingers into his ears and spitting touched his tongue and looking up to heaven groaned and said to him "*Ephphatha*" which is "Be opened."

His ears were opened, at once the block on his tongue was loosed and he spoke right.

He ordered them to tell nobody but the more he ordered the more wildly they declared it. They were wildly amazed saying "He has done everything right—he makes the deaf hear and the dumb speak."

In those days there was a big crowd again with nothing to eat and calling the disciples to him he said to them "I pity the crowd since they've been with me three days and have nothing to eat. If I send them off hungry to their homes they'll give out on the way—some of them are from far off."

His disciples answered him "Where could anyone get loaves to feed these people here in a desert?"

He asked them "How many loaves do you have?"

They said "Seven."

He ordered the crowd to lie back on the ground and taking the seven loaves and giving thanks he broke and gave to his disciples to serve.

They served the crowd.

They had a few little fish and blessing them he said for those to be served too.

They ate and were fed and took up seven trays of excess scraps—now they were about four thousand—

and he sent them off.

And at once embarking in the boat with his disciples he came to the region of Dalmanutha.

The Pharisees came out and began to debate with him, demanding from him a sign from heaven, tempting him.

Groaning in his spirit he said "Why does this generation demand a sign? Amen I tell you no sign will be given this generation!" And leaving them again, embarking he went off to the far side. They forgot to take bread—except for one loaf they had nothing with them in the boat—and he ordered them saying "Look, watch out for the Pharisees' leaven and Herod's leaven."

They argued with one another that they had no bread.

Knowing Jesus said to them "Why argue that you have no bread? Don't you see yet or understand? Have your hearts been hardened? *'Having eyes don't you see? Having ears don't you hear?'* Don't you remember? When I broke the five loaves for the five thousand how many basketsful of scraps did you take?"

They said to him "Twelve."

"When the seven for the four thousand how many trays filled with scraps did you take?"

They said "Seven."

He said to them "You still don't understand?"

They came to Bethsaida.

And they brought a blind man to him and begged him to touch him.

Taking the blind man's hand he led him out of the village and spitting in his eyes and laying hands on him he questioned him "Do you see anything?"

Looking up he said "I see men that look like trees walking."

So again he put his hands on his eyes.

Then he looked hard, was restored and saw everything clearly.

He sent him home saying "You may not go to the village."

And Jesus and his disciples went out to the villages of Caesarea Philippi. On the way he questioned his disciples saying to them "Who do men say I am?"

They told him saying " 'John the Baptist' and others 'Elijah' but others 'One of the prophets.' "

He questioned them "But you—who do you say I am?"

Answering Peter said to him "You are Messiah."

He warned them not to tell anyone about him and began to teach them that the Son of Man must endure many things and be refused by the elders, chief priests and scholars and be killed and after three days rise again—he said the thing plainly.

Peter taking him aside began to warn him.

But he turning round and seeing his disciples warned Peter and said "Get behind me, Satan, since you think not of God's things but men's things."

And calling the crowd to him with his disciples he said to them "If anyone wants to come after me let him disown himself and lift his cross and follow me for whoever wants to save his life shall lose it but whoever shall lose his life because of me and the good news shall save it. For how does it help a man to get the whole world and forfeit his soul? For what can a man give to redeem his soul? Whoever is ashamed of me in this adulterous and sinful generation the Son of Man shall also be ashamed of him when he comes in the glory of his Father with the holy angels." And he said to them

"Amen I tell you that there are some of those standing here who shall never know death till they see the reign of God come in power."

After six days Jesus took Peter, James and John and led them up into a high mountain by themselves alone. He was changed in shape before them and his clothes became a very shining white such as no bleacher on earth can whiten them. And Elijah appeared to them with Moses and they were talking with Jesus.

Speaking up Peter said to Jesus "Rabbi, it's good for us to be here. Let's make three tents—one for you, one for Moses and one for Elijah." He didn't know what he said—they were terrified.

There came a cloud covering them and there came a voice out of the cloud "This is My son, the loved one. Hear him."

Suddenly looking round they no longer saw anyone but only Jesus alone with themselves.

Coming down from the mountain he ordered them to tell no one the things they saw except when the Son of Man should rise from the dead.

They kept that word to themselves discussing what is "To rise from the dead." And they questioned him saying "Why do the scholars say that Elijah must come first?"

He said to them "Elijah in fact coming first shall restore everything. How has it been written of the Son of Man?—that he should endure much, suffer and be scorned? But I tell you that Elijah has come already and they did with him what they wanted as it was written of him."

And coming to the disciples they saw a big crowd round them and scholars arguing with them.

At once seeing him all the crowd were much stunned and running up greeted him.

He questioned them "What are you arguing with them?"

One of the crowd answered him "Teacher, I brought you my son who has a dumb spirit. Wherever it seizes him it flings him down and he foams and gnashes his teeth and goes stiff. I told your disciples to expel him but they couldn't."

Answering them he said "O unbelieving generation, how long shall I be with you? How long must I bear you? Bring him to me."

They brought him to him.

And seeing him at once the spirit convulsed him fiercely and falling to the ground he wallowed foaming.

He questioned his father "How long is it since this happened to him?"

He said "Since childhood. Often it throws him into fire and water to destroy him but if you can do anything take pity on us. Help us."

Jesus said to him " 'If you can'?—everything can be for a believer."

Crying out at once the child's father said "I believe! Help my unbelief."

Seeing a crowd running together Jesus warned the foul spirit saying to it "Dumb and deaf spirit, I order you come out of him and enter him no more!"

Screaming and convulsing him greatly it came out and he was lifeless so that many said he was dead.

But Jesus taking hold of his hand pulled him and he stood.

When he entered a house his disciples asked him privately "Why couldn't we expel it?"

He told them "This kind can come out only through prayer."

Leaving there they passed through Galilee. He wanted no one to know since he was teaching his disciples. He told them "The Son of Man is betrayed into men's hands. They shall kill him and being killed after three days he shall rise."

They were ignorant of the prophecy and afraid to ask him.

And they came to Capernaum and once in the house he questioned them "What were you discussing on the way?"

They were silent for on the way they had argued with one another who was greater.

Sitting he called the twelve and said to them "If anyone wishes to be first he shall be last of all and servant of all." Then taking a little child he set him in their midst and folding him in his arms he said to them "Whoever welcomes one little child like this in my name welcomes me and whoever welcomes me welcomes not me but the one who sent me."

John said to him "Teacher, we saw someone expelling demons in your name. We stopped him since he doesn't follow us."

But Jesus said "Don't stop him. No one will do a powerful thing in my name and soon speak evil of me. Whoever is not against us is for us and whoever gives you a cup of water to drink because you are Messiah's —Amen I tell you that he shall never lose his reward. And whoever causes one of these little ones who believe to sin, it would be better for him if a great millstone were set round his neck and he were thrown in the sea. If your hand makes you sin cut it off. It's better you enter life maimed than having two hands go off into Gehenna into unquenchable fire. If your foot makes you sin cut it off. It's better you enter life lame than having two feet be thrown into Gehenna. And if your eye makes you sin gouge it out. It's better you enter the reign of God one-eyed than having two eyes be thrown into Gehenna *'where their worm never dies and the fire is not quenched.'* For everyone shall be salted with fire. Salt is good but if salt goes bland how will you season it? Have salt in yourselves and keep peace with one another."

Rising from there he came to the fringes of Judea and the far side of Jordan. Crowds followed him again and as usual he taught them.

Coming up Pharisees questioned him if it was right for a man to reject his wife—testing him.

Answering he said to them "What did Moses command you?"

They said "Moses allowed us to write a notice of divorce and to dismiss her."

Jesus said to them "He wrote you this command for your hardheartedness. But from the start of creation *'He made them male and female and because of that a man shall leave his father and mother and the two shall be one flesh'* so that they're no longer two but one. Thus what God yoked man must not divide."

Back in the house the disciples questioned him about this.

He said to them "Whoever dismisses his wife and marries another commits adultery on her. And if she dismissing her husband marries another she commits adultery."

They brought him children to touch but the disciples warned them.

Seeing Jesus was indignant and said to them "Let the little children come to me—don't stop them—for the reign of God belongs to such. Amen I tell you whoever doesn't welcome the reign of God like a child shall never enter it." And folding them in his arms and putting his hands on them he blessed them.

As he went out onto the road a man ran up and kneeling to him asked him "Kind teacher, what must I do to inherit eternal life?"

Jesus said to him "Why do you call me *kind*? No one is kind but one—God. You know the commandments—'*do not kill, do not commit adultery, do not steal, do not give perjured witness,*' do not cheat, '*honor your father and mother.*'"

He said to him "Teacher, all these things I've kept since my youth."

Then Jesus gazing at him loved him and said to him "One thing is lacking you. Go sell what you have and give to the poor—you'll have treasure in heaven. Then come follow me."

But he was shocked by the word and went away grieving since he had great belongings.

Looking round Jesus said to his disciples "How strenuously the rich shall enter the reign of God!"

The disciples were stunned at his words.

But Jesus speaking again said to them "Sons, how strenuous it is to enter the reign of God! It's easier for a camel to go through a needle's eye than for a rich man to enter the reign of God."

They were much amazed saying to themselves "Who can be saved?"

Gazing at them Jesus said "With men it's impossible but not with God for everything is possible with God."

Peter started saying "Look, we left everything and followed you—"

But Jesus said "Amen I tell you there is no one who left home or brothers or sisters or mother or father or children or farms for my sake and the sake of the good news but shall get a hundredfold now in this time—houses and brothers and sisters and mothers and children and farms with persecutions—and in the age to come eternal life. Many first shall be last and last first."

They were on the road now going up to Jerusalem and Jesus was preceding them. They were stunned and the followers were afraid. Taking the twelve again he began to tell them the things about to happen to him—"Look, we're going up to Jerusalem and the Son of Man shall be handed to the chief priests and scholars. They'll condemn him to death and hand him to the Gentiles. They'll mock him, spit on him, flog him and kill him. Then after three days he'll rise again."

James and John—Zebedee's two sons—came up to him saying to him "Teacher, we want you to do whatever we ask for us."

He said to them "What do you want me to do for you?"

They said to him "Grant that one on your right and one on your left we may sit in your glory."

Jesus said "You don't know what you're asking. Can you drink the cup I'm drinking or be baptized with the baptism I'm to be baptized with?"

They said to him "We can."

And Jesus said to them "The cup I drink you'll drink and the baptism I'm baptized in you'll be baptized in. But to sit on my right or left is not mine to give, rather for the ones for whom it was prepared."

Hearing the ten began to be indignant at James and John.

So calling them to him Jesus said to them "You know that the self-styled rulers of the Gentiles lord it over them and their great men exercise power over them. But it's not so among you. Whoever among you wishes to be great shall be servant of all and whoever wishes to be first among you shall be slave of all for even the Son of Man didn't come to be served but to serve and give his life a ransom for many."

They got to Jericho and as he was leaving Jericho with his disciples and a sizable crowd Timeus' son— Bartimeus a blind man begging—sat by the road. Hearing that it was Jesus the Nazarene he began to cry out and say "Son of David, Jesus, pity me!"

Many warned him to be still but he cried out all the more "Son of David, pity me!"

Stopping Jesus said "Call him."

So they called the blind man saying to him "Cheer up. Stand. He's calling you."

Throwing off his coat and jumping up he came to Jesus.

Answering him Jesus said "What do you want me to do for you?"

The blind man said to him "Rabboni, to see."

Jesus said "Go. Your faith has cured you."

At once he saw and followed him in the road.

And as they neared Jerusalem at Bethphage and

Bethany toward the Mount of Olives he sent two of his disciples and told them "Go to the village opposite you and at once entering it you'll find a tethered colt on which no one has yet sat. Untie it and bring it. If anyone says to you 'Why are you doing this?' say 'The Lord needs it and will send it back at once."

They went and found a colt tied at a door outside in the street and they untied it.

Some of those standing there said to them "What are you doing untying the colt?"

They said to them what Jesus said.

So they let them go.

They brought the colt to Jesus and threw their coats on it.

He sat on it.

Many spread their coats in the road and others branches of leaves cut from the fields. The ones leading and the ones following cried out " 'Hosanna! Blessed he who comes in the Lord's name!' Blessed the coming reign of David our father! Hosanna in the heights!"

So he entered Jerusalem and the Temple and looking round at everything—the hour now being late—he went out to Bethany with the twelve.

On the next day as they went out from Bethany he hungered and seeing a figtree in the distance in leaf he went to see if maybe he could find something on it. Coming to it he found nothing but leaves since it was not the time for figs. Speaking out he said to it "Let no one—never again—eat fruit from you."

The disciples heard him.

Then they came to Jerusalem and entering the Temple he began to expel those selling and buying in the Temple. He upset the moneychangers' tables, the dovesellers' chairs and did not let anyone carry anything through the Temple. Then he taught and said to them "Hasn't it been written that '*My house shall be called a house of prayer for all nations*'? But you have made it '*a bandits' cave.*' "

The chief priests and scholars heard and looked for how they might destroy him since they feared him and all the crowd was amazed by his teaching.

When it was late they went out of the city.

And passing along early they saw the figtree withered from the roots.

Remembering Peter said to him "Rabbi, look. The figtree which you cursed has withered."

Answering Jesus said to them "Have faith in God. Amen I tell you that whoever says to this mountain 'Be raised and thrown into the sea' and has no doubts in his heart but believes that what he says is happening, it shall be his. So I tell you, all that you pray and ask for—believe that you get and it shall be yours. And when you stand praying forgive if you have anything against anyone so your Father in heaven may also forgive your sins."

They came again to Jerusalem and as he walked in the Temple the chief priests, scholars and elders came to him and said to him "By what right do you do these things? Or who gave you this right that you do these things?"

Jesus said to them "I'll ask you one word. Answer me and I'll tell you by what right I do these things. John's baptism—was it heaven's or men's? Answer me."

They argued among themselves saying "If we say 'Heaven's' he'll say 'Then why didn't you believe him?'

but if we say 'Men's' "—they feared the crowd for everybody held that John was certainly a prophet. So answering Jesus they said "We don't know."

Jesus said to them "Neither will I tell you by what right I do these things" and he started speaking to them in parables. "A man planted a vineyard and put a fence round it, dug a winevat and built a watchtower. Then he leased it to tenants and went far away. At the right season he sent a slave to the tenants to get some fruit from the vineyard. Taking him they beat him and sent him away empty. Again he sent them another slave. They struck him on the head and insulted him. So he sent another and they killed that one and many more, beating some, killing others. He had one left, a much-loved son. He sent him to them last saying 'They will honor my son.' But those tenants said to themselves 'This is the heir. Come let's kill him. The inheritance will be ours.' Taking him they killed him and flung him outside the vineyard. What will the lord of the vineyard do? He'll come, kill the tenants and give the vineyard to others. Haven't you read this text?

> *A stone which the builders rejected,*
>   *This became the keystone.*
> *This was from the Lord*
>   *And is wonderful in our eyes.*"

They longed to arrest him but feared the crowd since they knew he had told the parable on them. So leaving him they went away and sent to him some Pharisees and Herodians to snare him in a word.

Coming they said to him "Teacher, we know you're honest and that no one counts heavily with you since you don't regard men's faces but really teach God's way. Is it right to pay tribute to Caesar or not? Should we pay or not pay?"

But knowing their hypocrisy he said to them "Why tempt me? Bring me a denarius so I may see."

They brought one.

And he said to them "Whose picture is this and whose inscription?"

They told him "Caesar's."

So Jesus said to them "Caesar's things give back to Caesar and God's things to God."

They were dumbfounded by him.

Then Sadducees came to him who say there is no resurrection and asked him saying "Teacher, Moses wrote for us that if anyone's brother die and leave a wife and leave no child then his brother may take the wife and rear seed for his brother. There were seven brothers and the first got a wife and dying left no seed. The second got her and died not leaving seed and the third likewise. The seven left no seed. Last of all the woman died too. At the resurrection when they rise again which of them will she be wife to?—for the seven had her as wife."

Jesus said to them "Aren't you wrong in not knowing the scriptures or God's power?—for when they rise again from the dead they neither marry nor are given in marriage but are like angels in the heavens. But about the dead that they are raised—didn't you read in the scroll of Moses how at the bush God spoke to him saying '*I the God of Abraham, the God of Isaac, the God of Jacob*'? He's not the God of the dead but the living. You're deeply wrong."

One of the scholars approaching, hearing their dis-

cussion and knowing he answered them well asked him
"What commandment is first of all?"

Jesus answered "First is *'Hear, Israel, the Lord our
God is one Lord and you shall love the Lord your God
with all your heart, with all your soul and with all your
strength.'* Second, this—*'You shall love your neighbor
like yourself.'* There is no other commandment greater
than these."

The scholar said to him "True, Teacher. You say
rightly that there is One and no other beside Him and
to love Him with all the heart, with all the understanding and with all the strength and to love one's neighbor as oneself is more than all the burnt offerings and
sacrifices."

Jesus seeing that he answered wisely said to him
"You're not far from the reign of God."

Nobody dared question him further.

And going on as he taught in the Temple Jesus
said "How can the scholars say that Messiah is David's
son? David himself said through the Holy Spirit

> *The Lord said to my Lord*
> *'Sit at My right*
> > *Till I put your enemies under your feet.'*

David himself calls him Lord so how is he his son?"

The great crowd heard him gladly.

In his teaching he said "Beware of the scholars—
the ones liking to parade in flowing robes, to be greeted
in the markets, to have the best seats in synagogues
and the best places at banquets, the ones consuming
widows' houses under cover of long prayer: these shall
get greater damnation."

And sitting opposite the Treasury he saw how the

crowd put coppers into the Treasury. Many rich men put in much but one poor widow coming put in two lepta which make a penny. So calling his disciples to him he said to them "Amen I tell you that this poor widow put in more than all those contributing to the Treasury for they put in out of their surplus but this woman out of her need put in everything she had, all her goods."

When he went out of the Temple one of his disciples said to him "Teacher, look what stones, what buildings!"

Jesus said to him "See these great buildings? There shall surely be left no stone on stone which shall not surely be thrown down."

And when he sat on the Mount of Olives opposite the Temple, Peter, James, John and Andrew asked him privately "Tell us when all this will be and what will be the sign when all this is finished?"

So Jesus began to say to them "Watch so nobody leads you away. Many shall come in my name saying 'I am' and shall lead many away. But when you hear of wars and tales of wars don't be frightened. It must happen but the end won't be yet for nation shall be set against nation and kingdom against kingdom. There'll be earthquakes in places, there'll be famines—these are the onset of birth and pain. But see to yourselves. They'll hand you over to courts, you'll be beaten in synagogues, you'll stand before governors and kings for my sake to witness to them since the good news must first be announced to all nations. When they lead you out and hand you over don't worry yourself with what you'll say but what's given you in that hour say that for you're not the ones speaking but the Holy Spirit.

Brother shall hand brother over to death and a father his child, children shall rise against parents and kill them and you'll be hated by everyone because of my name but the one surviving to the end—that one shall be saved. Still when you see the desolating horror standing where it shouldn't"—let the reader understand—"then those in Judea let them flee to the mountains. Him on the roof let him not climb down or go in to take anything from his house. And him in the field let him not go back to the rear to take his coat. But woe to pregnant women and them suckling in those days. Pray for it not to happen in winter for those days shall be a trial such as has not come since the start of creation which God created till now and shall surely never come again. Unless the Lord shortened the days no flesh would be spared but because of the chosen whom He chose He shortened the days. So if anyone tells you 'Look here, the Messiah! Look there!' don't believe it. False Messiahs and false prophets shall appear and do signs and wonders to seduce the chosen if possible. But you, see!—I've warned you of everything. In those days after that trial the sun shall turn dark, the moon give none of her light. The stars shall be falling from heaven and the powers in the heavens shall quake. Then they'll see the Son of Man coming on clouds with great power and glory and then he'll send the angels and they'll gather his chosen from the four winds, from pole of earth to pole of heaven. Now learn a lesson from the figtree—when its branch is tender again and puts out leaves you know that summer is near. So too when you see these things happen know that he is at the doors. Amen I tell you that no way shall this generation pass till all these things happen.

Heaven and earth shall pass but my words shall not pass. But about that day or hour nobody knows— neither the angels in heaven nor the Son, only the Father. Watch. Stay awake for you don't know when the time is. It's like a traveler leaving his house and putting his slaves in charge each with his own work and he ordered the doorman to watch. You watch then since you don't know when the lord of the house is coming either late or at midnight or at cock-crow or early or coming suddenly he may find you sleeping. What I say to you I say to all—watch."

Now it was the Passover, the feast of unleavened bread, after two days and the chief priests and the scholars searched for how seizing him by deceit they might kill him for they said "Not at the feast or there'll be an outcry from the people."

When he was in Bethany in the house of Simon the leper as he lay back a woman came with an alabaster flask of costly pure nard ointment. Breaking the alabaster flask she poured it over his head. Some were indignant among themselves "Why has this waste of ointment occurred? This ointment could be sold for more than three hundred denarii and given to the wretched." They scolded her.

But Jesus said "Let her be. Why make trouble for her? She did a good deed on me. The wretched you always have with you and whenever you want you can do good to them but me you don't always have. What she could she did. She was early to anoint my body for burial. Amen I tell you wherever the good news is declared in all the world what this woman did shall also be told as a memory of her."

Then Judas Iscariot, one of the twelve, went to the

chief priests so he might betray him to them.

Hearing they were glad and promised to give him silver.

And he looked for how he might conveniently betray him.

On the first day of unleavened bread when they slaughtered the Passover lamb the disciples said to him "Where do you want us to go and arrange for you to eat the Passover?"

He sent two of his disciples and told them "Go into the city. You'll be met by a man carrying a water-jug. Follow him. Wherever he goes in tell the owner 'The teacher says "Where is my guestroom where I can eat the Passover with my disciples?" ' He'll show you a big room upstairs all spread and ready. Prepare for us there."

The disciples went out and entered the city and found it as he told them. Then they prepared the Passover.

As evening fell he came with the twelve and as they lay back and ate Jesus said "Amen I tell you that one of you shall betray me, the one eating with me."

They started grieving and saying to him one by one "Surely not I?"

He said to them "One of the twelve, him dipping with me in the common bowl. For the Son of Man is really going his way as was written of him but woe to the man through whom the Son of Man is betrayed. Better for him if that man were not born."

As they were eating he took a loaf and blessing it he broke and gave to them and said "Take. This is my body." And taking a cup and giving thanks he gave to them.

All drank of it.

He said to them "This is my blood of the covenant poured out for many. Amen I tell you never in any way will I drink of the fruit of the vine till that day when I drink it new in the reign of God."

After singing the hymn they went out to the Mount of Olives.

And Jesus said to them "All of you shall fall since it was written

> '*I will strike down the shepherd*
> *And the sheep shall be scattered.*'

But after I'm raised I'll go ahead of you to Galilee."

Peter said to him "Even if everybody stumbles not I."

Jesus said to him "Amen I tell you, you—today, tonight before the cock crows twice—you'll deny me three times."

But he just kept saying "If I must die with you no way would I deny you."

All said likewise too.

They came to a piece of land whose name was Gethsemane and he said to his disciples "Sit here while I pray." He took Peter, James and John with him and began to be deeply appalled and harrowed so he said to them "My soul is anguished to death. Stay here and watch." Going on a little he fell on the ground and prayed that if it were possible the hour might turn away and he said "*Abba*, Father, everything is possible to You. Take this cup from me—still not what I want but You." He came and found them sleeping and said to Peter "Simon are you sleeping? Couldn't you watch one hour? Watch and pray so you don't come to testing—oh the spirit is ready but the flesh is weak." Going off again he prayed saying the same words. Coming back he found them sleeping since their eyes were growing heavy and they didn't know how to answer him. He came the third time and said to them "Sleep now and rest. It's over. The hour came. Look, the Son of Man is betrayed into sinners' hands. Get up. Let's go. Look, the one who betrays me is nearing."

At once while he was still speaking Judas appeared—one of the twelve—and with him a crowd with swords and sticks from the chief priests, scholars and elders. The one betraying him had given them a sign saying "Whomever I kiss is he. Seize him and take him off securely." At once coming up to him he said "Rabbi!" and kissed him lovingly.

They got their hands on him and seized him.

But one of the bystanders drawing a sword struck the high priest's slave and cut off his ear.

Speaking out Jesus said to them "Did you come out with swords and sticks as if against a rebel to arrest me? Daily I was with you in the Temple teaching and you didn't seize me. But the scriptures must be done."

Deserting him they all ran.

One young man followed him dressed in a linen shirt over his naked body. They seized him but leaving the shirt behind he fled naked.

Then they took Jesus off to the high priest and all the chief priests, elders and scholars gathered.

Peter followed him far off right into the high priest's courtyard, sat with the servants and warmed himself by the blaze.

Now the chief priests and all the Sanhedrin looked for testimony against Jesus to execute him but they found none since many testified falsely against him and the testimonies were not the same. Some standing testified falsely against him saying "We heard him saying 'I'll tear down this Temple made by hand and after three days I'll build another not handmade.' " Even so their testimony was not consistent.

Standing in the center the high priest questioned Jesus saying "Won't you answer anything these men testify against you?"

But he was silent and answered nothing.

Again the high priest questioned him and said to him "You are Messiah, the son of the Blessed?"

Jesus said "I am and you shall see the Son of Man sitting at the right of Power and coming with clouds of heaven."

The high priest tearing his robes said "What further need do we have for witnesses? You heard the blasphemy. How does it look to you?"

They all condemned him worthy of death. Some began to spit at him, cover his face, hit him and say to him "Prophesy!" and the servants treated him to blows.

When Peter was down in the courtyard one of the high priest's maids came and seeing Peter warming himself she looked at him and said "You were with the Nazarene Jesus."

But he denied it saying "I don't know him or understand what you're saying." Then he went out into the porch and the cock crowed.

Seeing him the maid began again to say to those standing round "This man is one of them."

But again he denied it.

After a little again those standing round said to Peter "Surely you're one of them. It's plain you're a Galilean."

He began to curse himself and swear "I don't know this man you mention." At once a second time a cock crowed and Peter remembered the word Jesus said to him "Before the cock crows twice you'll deny me three times" and dwelling on that he wept.

At once in the morning the chief priests held council with the elders, scholars and all the Sanhedrin and binding Jesus they led him off and handed him to Pilate.

Pilate asked him "You're the king of the Jews?"

Answering him he said "You say."

The chief priests charged him with many things.

But Pilate asked him again "Will you answer nothing? See how much they charge you with."

But Jesus still answered nothing.

Pilate wondered.

At each feast he freed for them one prisoner they requested. There was one named Barabbas held with the rebels who had committed murder in the rebellion. So the crowd came up and began to ask for his usual act.

But Pilate answered them saying "Do you want me to free you the king of the Jews?"—he knew the chief priests had handed him over out of envy.

But the chief priests incited the crowd to free them Barabbas instead.

So Pilate spoke out again to them "What must I do then with the one you call king of the Jews?"

They shouted back "Crucify him!"

But Pilate said to them "Why? What evil has he done?"

They shouted louder "Crucify him!"

Then Pilate wanting to pacify the crowd freed them Barabbas and handed over Jesus having flogged him so he could be crucified.

The soldiers led him off into the courtyard called Pretorium and summoned the whole cohort. They put on him a purple robe and plaiting a thorn crown they put it round him. Then they started saluting him "Hail, king of the Jews!" They hit his head with a reed, spat on him and kneeling down worshipped him. When they had mocked him they took the purple off him and put on his own clothes. Then they led him out to crucify him. They forced one Simon—a Cyrenean from the country, the father of Alexander and Rufus— to carry his cross. So they brought him to the place Golgotha which means "Skull Place." They gave him wine drugged with myrrh but he would not take it. Then they crucified him and divided his clothes casting lots for them, what each might take. It was nine in the morning when they crucified him. The notice of the charge against him was written above "The King of the Jews." With him they crucified two thieves one on his right and one on his left.

Those passing by insulted him wagging their heads and saying "So! The one who would destroy the Temple and build it in three days! Save yourself. Get down off the cross."

In the same way the chief priests joking with each other and with the scholars said "He saved others. He can't save himself! Messiah king of Israel!—let him get down off the cross so we can see and believe."

And those crucified with him reviled him.

At noon darkness came over the whole land till three and at three Jesus shouted in a loud voice " *'Eloi, Eloi, lama sabachthani?'* " which means "My God, my God, why did You forsake me?"

Some of the bystanders hearing said "Look, he's calling Elijah" and running one filled a sponge with vinegar and putting it round a stick gave him to drink saying "Let him be. Let's see if Elijah comes to take him down."

But Jesus giving a loud cry breathed his last.

The Temple curtain was torn in two from top to bottom.

The centurion standing opposite seeing that he breathed his last that way said "Surely this man was son of God."

There were women too at a distance watching among whom were both Mary the Magdalene, Mary the mother of the younger James and mother of Joses, and Salome who followed him when he was in Galilee and served him and many others who had come up with him to Jerusalem.

Now when evening came since it was preparation which is the day before the sabbath Joseph from Arimathea, an important councilor who was himself also expecting the reign of God, came and boldly went in to Pilate and asked for Jesus' body.

Pilate wondered if he was already dead and summoning the centurion questioned him how long ago he died. Then learning from the centurion he presented the corpse to Joseph.

Having bought new linen and taken him down he wrapped him with the linen, put him in a tomb hewn from rock and rolled a stone across the entrance of the tomb.

Mary the Magdalene and Mary the mother of Joses watched where he was put.

When the sabbath passed Mary the Magdalene, Mary the mother of James, and Salome bought spices so they could come and anoint him. Very early on the first day of the week they came to the tomb as the sun was rising. They said to each other "Who'll roll the stone off the tomb door for us?" and looking up they saw the stone had been rolled back for it was huge. Entering the tomb they saw a young man sitting on the right dressed in a white robe and they were much stunned.

But he said to them "Don't be stunned. Are you looking for Jesus the crucified Nazarene? He was raised. He isn't here. Look, the place where they laid him. But go tell his disciples and Peter 'He's going ahead of you to Galilee. There you'll see him as he told you.'"

Going out they fled the tomb—they were shuddering and wild—and they told no one anything for they were afraid.

I saw a new heaven and a new earth for the first heaven and the first earth were vanished and the sea was no more. And I saw the holy city New Jerusalem descending out of heaven from God readied like a bride decked for her husband. And I heard a loud voice from the throne saying "Look, God's tent is with men. He shall tent with them, they shall be His people, God Himself shall be with them and wipe every tear from their eyes and death shall be no more nor grief nor crying nor pain no more since the old things are vanished."

And He who sits on the throne said "Look, I make all new." And He said "Write, since these words are credible and true." And He said to me "It is done. I am the Alpha and the Omega, the start and the finish. I will give to the thirsty from the spring of life's water freely. The victor shall inherit all this and I will be God to him and he shall be son to Me but to fearers and faithless and monsters and murderers and whorechasers and wizards and idolaters and the false—their part in the lake which burns with fire and sulphur which is second death."

And one of the seven angels that have the seven bowls full of seven last plagues came to me and spoke with me saying "Come I will show you the Bride, the Lamb's wife."

Then he took me off in spirit to a great high

mountain and showed me the city holy Jerusalem descending out of heaven from God, having God's glory. Her shining was like most precious stone, like jasper stone crystalline having also a great high wall having twelve gates and at the gates twelve angels and names inscribed which are of the twelve tribes of Israel's sons—on the east three gates, on the north three gates, on the south three gates, on the west three gates and the wall of the city having twelve foundations and on them names of the Lamb's twelve apostles. The one speaking with me had a golden stick to measure the city, its gates and its wall. The city lies foursquare and its length is also as much as its breadth. He measured the city with the stick—twelve thousand furlongs: the length and breadth and height of it are equal. He measured its wall, a hundred forty-four cubits, man's measure—that is angel's. The structure of its wall was jasper and the city was gold—pure like pure glass—and the foundations of the wall of the city were adorned with every precious stone: the first foundation jasper, the second sapphire, the third chalcedony, the fourth emerald, the fifth sardonyx, the sixth carnelian, the seventh chrysolite, the eighth beryl, the ninth topaz, the tenth chrysoprase, the eleventh turquoise, the twelfth amethyst. The twelve gates were twelve pearls—each of the gates was itself one pearl—and the street of the city was gold pure as clear glass. I saw no temple in it for the Lord God Almighty is its temple and the Lamb. And the city has no need of the sun or the moon to shine in it for God's glory lights it and its lamp is the Lamb. The nations shall walk by its light and the kings of the earth bring their glory to it and its gates shall never be shut by day for there'll be no night—they'll bring the glory and honor of the nations to it. Anything unclean may never come in doing foulness and lying but those who are written in the Lamb's scroll of life. And he showed me a river of life's water bright as crystal flowing from the throne of God and the Lamb down the middle of its street. And on either side of the river—a tree of life bearing twelve fruits, yielding its fruit each month and the leaves of the tree are for healing the nations (every curse shall be no more). The throne of God and the Lamb shall be in it and His slaves shall serve Him and see His face—His name on their foreheads. Night shall be no more and they have no need of lamplight and sunlight since Lord God lights them and they shall reign to the ages of the ages.

Then he said to me "These words are credible and true and Lord God of the spirits of the prophets sent His angel to show His slaves what must happen soon. 'Look, I am coming soon. Happy is he who keeps the words of the prophecy of this scroll.' "

And I John—the one seeing and hearing all this—when I heard and saw fell down to worship at the feet of the angel showing me all this.

But he said to me "See! No! I am a fellow slave with you and your brothers the prophets and with them who keep the words of this scroll. Worship God." And he said to me "Do not seal the words of the prophecy of this scroll since the time is close. The unjust let him be unjust still. And the filthy let him be filthy still. And the just let him be just still. And the holy let him be holy still. 'Look, I am coming soon and My wage is with Me to give to each according to his work. I am the Alpha and the Omega, I the first and

the last, start and finish. Happy the ones who wash
their robes. That shall be their right to the tree of life
and they shall enter the city through the gates—but
outside the dogs and the wizards and the whorechasers
and the murderers and the idolaters and all who love
and practice lying. I Jesus sent My angel to witness for
you all this in the churches. I am the root and child of
David—the bright, the morning star.' "

And the Spirit and the Bride said "Come!"

And the one who hears let him say "Come!" And
the parched let him come—the yearning—and take
life's water freely.

I witness to all hearing the words of the prophecy
of this scroll. If anyone adds to them God will add to
him the plagues that are written in this scroll and if
anyone subtracts from the words of the scroll God shall
take from him his share in the tree of life and the Holy
City, things written in this scroll.

Says He who witnesses all this "Yes I am coming
soon."

Amen. Come Lord Jesus.

The grace of the Lord Jesus Christ with all.

Born in Macon, North Carolina, Reynolds Price studied at Duke University and at Merton College, Oxford University where he was a Rhodes Scholar. In 1962, his first novel, *A Long and Happy Life*, received the William Faulkner Foundation Award. He has since published ten novels, as well as volumes of short stories, poetry, essays, and autobiography. A member of the American Academy of Arts and Letters (from which he has received an Award in Literature), he teaches at Duke University where he is James B. Duke Professor of English.